LONE ADVENTURER

LONE ADVENTURER

The Story of Sir Francis Chichester

JOHN ROWLAND

ROY PUBLISHERS, INC.
NEW YORK 10021

Library of Congress Number 69-12123

PRINTED IN GREAT BRITAIN

To
Fytton and Barbara
*to provide a souvenir of certain
events of May, 1968*

CONTENTS

CHAPTER ONE

THE YOUNG CHICHESTER

WITH many people who become famous, it is possible to see from their youngest days the destiny that they are to fulfil. The boy who was one day to become Sir Francis Chichester might be thought to be one of them, since his earliest days in Devon show him as an adventurous boy, and adventure was to be the keynote of his life. In his own story of his life he described what he still thinks was his first great adventure. He was walking in the woods near his home, eleven years old, a schoolboy with very marked ideas of his own. He saw a viper curling away through the grass. A country boy, he was not afraid of snakes, and he grabbed this viper by the tail. He pushed it into a handkerchief which he had dragged from his pocket, and then set out for home.

On the way home he had to cross a field, and here he saw a lazy-looking beetle warming himself in the sun. He thought that the snake might be a bit hungry. He remembered that snakes often fed on sizeable creatures, so he untied the handkerchief and tried to give the snake a feed of tasty beetle. The snake took no notice of the beetle. Instead, it looked at the boy who had captured it, curled itself up, and hissed fiercely at him.

Francis Chichester thought that this was a pretty ungrateful sort of snake. It had been given a chance of a good feed, and it did not seem to want to eat, after all. So he made to push it back into its temporary prison in his handkerchief. Suddenly, without any warning, the snake struck at him and bit him on the finger. "It stung like six wasp stings," Francis wrote many years later. It was a highly unpleasant business, and the pain was quite terrifying.

He sucked at the wound. Then he hurried home as best he could. But already his hand was swelling, and by the time he reached home the swelling had begun to go up his arm. On the way he had met a farmer, who had killed the snake. Francis, in spite of the bite, had wrapped it up in the handkerchief again. He still intended to take it home.

That home was some four miles from the North Devon town of Barnstaple, on the River Taw. Francis's father did not appear very alarmed that his son had been bitten by a snake, and simply told him to get out his bicycle and go off to the hospital in Barnstaple, where the bite would be treated. His father followed with a horse and trap.

At the hospital, when they sliced open the wound to remove the poison, Francis fainted. For some hours, indeed, his life was in danger. But when he had recovered and had been sent home once more, he was rather proud that the local newspapers reported this incident. It was his first taste of newspaper publicity. In the years to come he was to make news in papers all over the world, to be reported on radio programmes and seen on television screens. But never again did he get quite as much satisfaction from these things as he did from seeing that Devonshire paper with the news of his first real adventure.

His childhood, indeed, had been rather unusual. When he was seven he had gone to a school some miles from his home. When very young he had acquired the habit of wandering about the countryside, studying wild creatures and wild plants. Insects, birds, field-mice—and snakes!—were among his greatest interest, and some of the subjects that he had to study at school seemed fairly dull compared to the exciting creatures he saw roaming in the Devonshire woods and fields. For a long time he was something of a rebel in school, and punishment often came his way. A boy who does not quite fit into the ordinary pattern of school life often gets into trouble, and Francis Chichester was no exception to this rule.

Soon, however, he was sent to a school at Bournemouth, and here he felt much happier and much more at home. More than anything he loved going down to the sea to bathe. It was from this moment that he started on that love of the sea which was to be one of the greatest things in his life. One day the school played a cricket match against the boys from a naval training ship. It was all very exciting; and as he lay in his bed, overlooking the sea, Francis could see the lights of the ship as it lay at anchor.

The Bournemouth school was only for young boys. Francis had been very happy there; but the years passed all too swiftly for him, and soon he was sent to the famous public school of Marlborough, which was a very different place. At Bournemouth he had finished as captain of the cricket team and head of the school. At Marlborough he was to find himself a very unimportant little boy, a junior who knew nothing of school customs and traditions. From being a very prominent person, he sank, suddenly, to being the lowest of the low—a new boy in the bottom form.

This was, too, in the days of the First World War, when food was scarce. The discipline of the school was harsh, and the food Francis found terrible. He was, to begin with, very unhappy there.

The school was high up on the Marlborough Downs, and in winter it was bitterly cold. There was one huge room where about 200 boys used to congregate when they were not actually in classes, and this room had two big fires. But there was a school habit that only the bigger and more senior boys were allowed to get near to the fire, which meant that the juniors stood well away from the fire and shivered. When Francis had been home for the summer holidays, and had to go back to Marlborough in September, he used to dread the long haul to Christmas. He kept a little calendar in his pocket, and crossed off the days, which seemed as if they would never pass.

In the summer things were a little better. Cricket was not compulsory, and the boys, if they did not want to play games, were permitted to go off on their own for rambles and walks, within ten miles from the school. Francis was delighted when he found that he could get to Upavon, where there was an aerodrome. He would lie in the field near the runway and watch the rather primitive machines of those days taking off and landing.

It was his spell by the seaside at Bournemouth which had first given him his love of the sea and ships. It was these visits to the Upavon aerodrome that gave him his other love—the love of flying. Those two loves would be with him for the whole of his life. In those early days he was not able to foresee this; all that he knew on those summer afternoons at Upavon was that flying was one of the most fascinating things that he had ever seen.

But it was not only aeroplanes that interested him. His early love of nature went on, and he still delighted to sit out and watch the wild life of the Downs. He also soon became very keen on Rugby football, and had a great ambition to get a place in the school fifteen. It was during this time that the New Zealand "All Blacks" were in Britain. They had a revolutionary idea, playing seven forwards instead of eight, so getting an extra man to take part in the swift passing movements outside the scrum. Francis suggested to the captain of the First Fifteen that the school team should try this out, and see if it would lead to as great success in school games as the New Zealand team had in the international sphere. At this time Francis had got his first chance to play for the school as a forward; but when only seven forwards were required, he lost his place. The extra place outside the scrum went, of course, to a player more accustomed to playing as a back.

He had physical drawbacks in playing Rugby. His sight was not good; he already wore spectacles, and as he had to leave these off on the football field, if the ball was kicked high in the air he could not see it. On one occasion, indeed, he was seen to run like fury in the wrong direction, away from the spot at which the ball eventually came to earth.

All the time, however, Francis was growing strong and wiry, and his brain was steadily improving. He was never very much the orthodox "swot" on whom so many schoolboys look down in disgust, but there were certain subjects at school which he found interesting. He was delighted, one term, therefore, to learn that in future boys were to be allowed to specialize in the subjects which interested them most. They would then be able to do a lot of extra work on these subjects, and to spend less time on the subjects which they did not like, or for which they were not really suited. This scheme held out all sorts of possibilities for this boy whose mind was working in a particular direction, for it would enable him to devote more time to things which would be useful to him in later life.

By the time that this scheme was introduced, Francis had become interested in engineering—especially aircraft engineering. And he thought that the school subject that would be most valuable to someone who wanted to be an engineer was mathematics. After all, all engines and machines are based on figures and drawings, and the subject that dealt with figures and drawings would thus be of the greatest possible value.

As he had been making his way up the school, the First World War had been fought. Many of the younger masters left, in order to join the armed forces. Older men, who had retired, came back and started teaching again, when they thought that they had completely finished with the job. But the work of the school went on with some smoothness. The war did not interfere very much with the day-to-day routine of teaching and learning. The food, as has been said, was not good. But there was a shortage of food felt by most people. Those at home felt the pinch as much as those who were away at a boarding school.

So, as Francis Chichester slogged away at his mathematics, world-shattering events went on across the channel. To begin with, he found specializing in mathematics very fascinating. A special form had been created for the purpose of mathematics study. There were about thirty boys in this form. But as the days went by, Francis slowly began to wonder if he had made a mistake in his decision to spend nearly all his time doing geometry and algebra. What had, to begin with, seemed so wonderful and so fascinating began to appear boring and difficult.

Day after day he found his interest in the subject getting less.

Of the thirty boys in the class, when the first examination came along, he was eleventh. Some boys would have thought that this was quite good—it was in the top half of the class, after all. But Francis was by no means satisfied with it. He told himself that there were ten boys there who were better at mathematics than he was. He thought that they were better than he would ever be. What was the use? he would ask himself. Why go slogging away at something that got more and more boring, when it was not really getting him anywhere at all?

For a time he told no one of his feelings. He got what pleasure he could obtain from wandering around the countryside, watching the wild birds and the little creatures which scurried out of the hedge and across the road. Then, after an hour or two of this, wandering about the country with the wind blowing through his hair, he would be back again in the classroom, working on the horrible problems of algebra which he never seemed able to get right.

It was a frustrating time of life. He was getting older, too—now he was very nearly grown up. Yet he was pinned down to a school routine that was getting almost impossible for him to stick.

Even the delight of going to Upavon and watching the aeroplanes was not enough to compensate for the utter frustration of the hours and hours that he had to spend over his mathematical lessons. But what could he do? It is never easy for a senior schoolboy to revolt against what the school is trying to teach him. This is especially so when it is a very famous school, and when his father is spending a lot of money in school fees to keep him there.

Even his dreams of being an aircraft engineer were being in a way thrown away, because his father had made no secret of the fact that he wanted Francis to go to a university, and then into the Indian Civil Service. In those days the Indian Civil Service, with the more important posts all filled by Englishmen, offered a very well-paid career. It offered security, too, for there were good pensions at the end of a period of service.

Francis did not want security. He wanted adventure. But where the adventure was to be found he did not know.

It was the winter term of 1918 when his feelings came to a head. He had not thought very much about the war, now staggering to its end. He had somehow taken it for granted that it would be over before he was old enough to be required to take any active part in it.

Then, in 1918, one of the worst influenza epidemics ever known struck right across Europe. A boarding school, of course, is a place where any infectious disease, when once it gets in, spreads very quickly. One or two cases appeared early in that term—and then boy after boy went down with it. High temperature, headache, limbs stiff and painful—the symptoms were unmistakable. The only thing to do with a boy who caught the disease was to take him to the sanatorium. The beds were soon filled. Mattresses were laid down on the floor, and the newcomers to the sanatorium were put on them. Soon even these were full, and row upon row of influenza victims lay on the floor.

Francis Chichester caught the disease, as did most of his friends. One or two of them died, and a large number were quite seriously ill.

During his time of recovery, lying there on a mattress and gradually getting back his strength, Francis Chichester had time to think. He thought about his sense of boredom during the hours and hours of mathematics that he had undergone. He thought of the fact that, if his father's ambition for him was to be achieved, he might have several years of this sort of thing ahead, at school or in college. It seemed to him that this was something too dreadful to contemplate.

When the armistice ending the war was signed—on November 11, 1918—he was too weak even to raise himself on his elbow and look out of the window of the sanatorium. He could hear cheers from outside, as the news spread. The war was at an end. But he had his little private war still to fight—the war against mathematics. How could he manage to fight it?

There was only one way, he told himself. He would have to leave Marlborough. And he would have to leave quickly, before he was again swallowed up by the daily mathematical routine.

It was not long, of course, from the end of term, when he would be going home for the Christmas holiday. In fact, by the time he made anything like a complete recovery from influenza, Christmas was nearly there. This was the time to break the news to his father.

Before getting the train for home he had seen his housemaster and the headmaster, had told them that he would not be coming back in January. He had therefore burnt his boats before breaking the news to his father.

It was with some trembling that he faced his father on the first day of the holidays.

"I want to tell you something," he said.

"All right. What is it?" his father asked.

"I've left Marlborough."

Silence.

"I said that I've left Marlborough."

Then the storm broke. "What do you mean?" his father said in icy tones.

"I mean that I have seen the head and my housemaster and told them that I shall not be coming back next month."

"*You've* told them? *You've* told them? Do *you* pay the fees?"

"No, Father."

"Don't you think that you owed it to me to ask my permission, at least, before doing this?"

"I'm sorry, Father, perhaps I ought to have asked you."

He could not say that he had done it in the way that he had because he was afraid that his father would have refused permission. He could not, though he tried, explain that he was getting more and more weary at the classroom routine, and that a further period of mathematics would drive him crazy. He could not say that he was appalled at the idea of three or four years at a university, just extending the knowledge which he had lately found it so difficult to acquire at school.

This was one of the most painful interviews in all Francis Chichester's life. He was fond of his father, as his father was of him, but it was impossible for either of them to make the other understand what was happening. Francis was resolved no longer to spend his hours at a desk, working on mathematical problems. His father was resolved to show him that he was throwing away an opportunity of an interesting and worth-while career in life. Neither, in actual fact, could make any impression on the other. But in the end, it was Francis who won this battle, as he was to win many more later on. His sheer determination won this battle—again as with many others. For he had made up his mind that he would not go back to Marlborough in January. And when Francis Chichester made up his mind, it stayed that way.

To study for years and then to go out and sit at an office desk in Bombay or Calcutta did not seem to him to be a proper life. It was, at all events, not the life that he wanted to lead. So his father had to agree that the boy should not go back to school.

CHAPTER TWO

CHANGE OF SCENE

IN THOSE days, just after the First World War, many
adventure-loving boys sought satisfaction by leaving
Britain and getting a job in the great overseas Dominions.
It was not always easy to get a job—it was not always even
easy to get a passage on a ship without a lengthy wait.
People who had been over in the British Isles to help in
the war effort were trying to get home; some of the great
ships were being used as troopships, to take soldiers back
to Australia or New Zealand. As a result of all this, the
ordinary person who wanted to book for a journey half-
way around the world often had to book months ahead.

Francis, when once he had made up his mind to leave
school, and had faced the wrath of his father, thought
that one of these overseas posts would be his passport to
adventure. Since he came from a country background,
perhaps a job on a farm would be the best thing at which
to aim.

But . . . where? There were many talks with his father
about this. In the end, they decided that New Zealand
was the place which held out the best prospects, and
which, at the same time, seemed attractive to Francis as a
country. What really turned the scales in favour of New
Zealand was when Francis met a New Zealand soldier
who was soon going back home. He sang the praises of his
native country so warmly that Francis Chichester had

little doubt that this was the country where he would be able to settle down most happily.

Unfortunately, there was the problem of finding his way there. Ships were booked up, as has been seen, for a long time ahead. And meanwhile Francis had to get something to do.

"You'd better get a job on a farm in England," his father advised him.

"But where?" Francis said.

"We'll have a look at advertisements. If you're going to do some sort of farming work in New Zealand, experience on a farm in England can't do you any harm. I don't suppose that conditions in the two countries are all that different," his father said sapiently.

So, after writing replies to a number of advertisements, Francis went off to work on a farm in Leicestershire. He worked there for several months, being paid five shillings a week. He learned a lot of the routine jobs, milking and feeding cows, spreading manure on the fields, and doing all kinds of odd tasks. He was not very happy there, and he found the work hard and the days long. But all the same he was able to tell himself that he was gaining experience that would be very useful to him in the days ahead.

He was very miserable when he caught the unpleasant disease of ringworm from one of the calves. This brings painful sores, especially on the head, and for some time he could not rid himself of these.

In those days there was a famous airship, called the R 34. One day, while Francis was in a field hoeing turnips, and resting his aching back whenever opportunity offered, he saw this strange cigar-shaped object floating across the sky. He was all alone in the field, and he rested on his hoe and watched it. Something of the interest in flying, which had been so much with them in those days at Upavon, seemed to revive.

Francis had never been especially happy on that Midland farm, and after about seven months there he was dismissed. This was because he had been returning from delivering a cargo of milk at the station, and got into a race on the way home. The churns of milk had been on a cart, drawn by a big horse. Another young man from a nearby farm had been doing a similar job for his master, and the two young men raced each other down a lane, whipping their horses into a fine frenzy of excitement. One wheel of the cart hit a large stone. The empty churns with which the cart was loaded went flying through the air. Francis was flung off his seat, but not much hurt. The horse, alarmed at the noise, galloped furiously on, through the bars of two gates, and ended up in the garden before the farm-house.

It was not surprising that Francis was sacked on the spot. He was scared, because a dog belonging to the farmer, alarmed at all the noise, had bitten his wrist. There had been some cases of rabies mentioned in the newspapers, and Francis knew that this disease, which human beings can catch as a result of a dog-bite, was very painful and very dangerous. His wrist throbbed, and he wondered if he had caught it. He was afraid to go home, since he thought his father might be very annoyed at him for having lost his job so soon.

However, he did get home, though he thought of getting some new post not too far away. One day he cycled to Exeter to apply for a job at a garage there. The round journey, which he did in one day, was ninety miles; and he did not get the job.

He lived for the day when he would be setting off for New Zealand, and one day in 1919 the great change took place. He had a working passage on an old German ship, called the *Bremen*, which the British had captured during the war, and he joined this ship at Plymouth. Plymouth, indeed, was to play a great part, at intervals, in his life, for it was from Plymouth Sound, nearly fifty years later, that he was to set off on the greatest of his voyages. But in 1919 all that was hidden in the mist of the future. In 1919 he felt a sense of adventure, in that he was setting off for an unknown country, where he knew only one human being—the sergeant whom he had met a few months before.

He was in part working his passage, which meant that he had to do tough jobs like shovelling coal. The crew were a very tough lot. The work was hard, which meant that at mealtimes everyone was ravenously hungry. There were often fights over the food. Francis's father had given him ten pounds in golden sovereigns as a parting gift, and this he kept in a belt, which was worn night and day. There might be thieves among the crew, he told himself, and this precious ten pounds had to be guarded at all costs.

At Wellington he got his discharge from the ship. His work had been good, and he was paid nine pounds for his help on the voyage. With nineteen pounds in his purse, he felt quite rich. But he had to get work pretty quickly, if he was not to starve. He had kept the address of the New Zealand sergeant, Ned Holmes, and Ned's father was a farmer on a fairly big scale. On one of his farms, near a place called Masterton, young Francis started work at a wage of ten shillings a week. This was twice as much as he had been paid on that farm back in Leicestershire, so he did not think he was being too badly done by.

This was a sheep farm, and Francis was given a job under the manager, who was a wonderful shepherd. After three weeks, however, he was dismissed, as the manager thought, with his poor sight, even assisted by glasses, he would not be able to watch the sheep in distant spots. Actually, Francis's sight, when he was wearing his glasses, was not at all bad, and he wondered if there was some other reason for his dismissal. He soon landed another job at a sheep station. But this was in a very isolated spot, nearly forty miles from Masterton, which was the nearest town.

This was a very hard job. The sheep station was 2,000 acres in extent, and there were over 3,000 sheep to look after, as well as a smaller number of cattle. To look after this vast herd there were two men, of whom Francis was now one! He had to ride everywhere, and spent most of the day on horseback. There were dogs, who helped in rounding up the sheep when required, and at shearing time, when the wool was cut off the backs of the sheep the two men, and their boss, worked all the hours of daylight.

As they were so isolated, they had to do their own cooking. The boss baked the bread. One day he suggested that Francis should have a shot at baking; but he baked the bread too much, and it was so hard that they were not able to eat it.

The boss was a very tidy man, which at that time Francis was not. He remembered, years afterwards, the look on his employer's face when he returned after a few days away, and found nearly a week's dirty dishes waiting to be washed up.

Francis soon got used to the routine of the sheep station. He loved riding, and to spend hours every day in the saddle gave him great joy. He was invited to a dance one evening, and he rode to the dance, forty-five miles, and back afterwards. It was a journey as long as that cycle-ride to Exeter and back to North Devon which he had done not so long before, but half the world away. It seemed as if it had taken place years before, so much change had come into his life in a matter of a few short months.

What he found less enjoyable was the work of moving sheep about. He found that sheep were stubborn and obstinate animals, and when he had to move 500 of them from one place to another, it was the most trying task that he had ever carried out in his life. He was once told of a neighbouring sheep station where one sheep had fallen into a deep ravine, and nearly 500 more had followed him, until the whole flock lay dead at the bottom.

This job was bringing him fifteen shillings a week. He thought it was worth more. He asked for a rise to twenty-five shillings a week, and was offered a pound a week. He decided that this was not enough, and looked around for different work. Soon he secured a post on a farm at a place called Taihape at £2 10s. a week. They asked him if he had done any milking, and he said that he had not. This was because he disliked the smell of milk. He had, in actual fact, done much milking in his Leicestershire days. He was glad that he had pretended to know nothing about it, when he heard others, who were doing the milking, getting up very early in the morning, whereas he did not have to start work until eight o'clock.

This farm was more mixed than any he had worked on before. There were a lot of cattle and many sheep. He still had to work with sheep and also look after cattle. One job that he especially enjoyed was sawing up wood. There had been many trees on the farm, which had not long ago been wild country, and the trees, when felled, had to be sawn up. Francis did a good deal of this work. It made him ravenously hungry—even hungrier than when he had been working in the stokehold of the ship. He told, years afterwards, stories of the meals he used to eat in those days. The normal breakfast, for example, consisted of a huge plate of porridge, a pound of steak with three fried eggs, and bread, butter and jam to finish off!

He became quite an expert sheep-shearer. He could manage to shear as many as seventy-five sheep a day. This, however, was a poor effort compared to the champions. Some men could tackle as many as 400 in a day.

By this time Francis had saved a bit of money. He had, too, got a new kind of ambition. He wanted to become an author. He felt lonely on the farm. He enjoyed much of the work, and it was pretty well paid by the standards of those days; but the other men did not seem to be very interested in anything but sheep and cattle, and if Francis spoke of some great author whose writing he admired, they just stared at him blankly. They had clearly never read many books.

So one day he studied his bank-book and his wallet, decided that he had enough money in hand to keep himself for a little while, and thought that he would try his hand at writing. He had got a little book which was supposed to teach anyone to write saleable short stories. Armed with this, and his little store of money, he left his job, and took lodgings in a nearby country town. Here he would sit with a pile of paper in front of him, and try to write. But he soon knew that this was not to be. He was still, of course, very young. Although he had travelled across the world, he had not enough knowledge of people and the way they lived. And he knew little if anything about the way in which professional writers set to work. Soon he sat glumly in his little room and told himself that he would never succeed in being a worth-while writer. But what on earth could he do?

The lone adventurer was faced with the sort of problem that comes to everyone who finds his work difficult and frustrating, who wants to get somewhere in life, but is not sure just where that is.

New Zealand consists of two large islands. Up to now Francis had spent the whole of his time in that distant land on North Island. He wondered if his luck would change if he changed his background. He still had a little money left; so he crossed on the steamer from North Island to South Island, and began to look around for a new sort of job there.

He had enjoyed working the saw-mill in his last job, and he wondered whether something in the timber trade might not bring him some more satisfaction than sheep-farming had done. Soon he landed a post with a firm who owned much forest land, which they were gradually felling, then disposing of the timber. Their offices were at Greymouth, on the west coast of South Island, but they were working on a forest which was miles away, at the end of a primitive railway, which at that time extended about ten miles out into the bush, surrounded by huge trees.

This railway was being gradually extended further away from Greymouth, and a gang of men were working on this extension. His first job with this company was in this gang. This, again, meant hard work, especially in clearing away tall trees that had to be felled to make way for the railway track. But Francis Chichester was never afraid of hard work of any kind, on land or sea.

Again, as with his work on the sheep farms, he felt lonely. The other men did not, as we say, speak his language. They all spoke English, of course, but there were many things that Francis was interested in which did not seem to interest them at all. So he felt cut off from friends and almost alone in a strange world of high trees and bush.

But then there came another chance for adventure. He heard that gold had been found not very far away. A strike of gold sometimes leads to something like a stampede; gold is a very valuable thing, and men are prepared to do almost anything to get it. When a new source of gold is found, there are often thousands of men who rush off to try to get hold of some of it.

So when Francis heard of this strike of gold, he packed his few belongings into a bag, humped this on his shoulder, and set off to walk into the direction of the new source of the precious metal.

On the way there he passed a gold-mine which was already being worked, and then set off into the forest, where he almost at once got lost. It was a very nasty moment. Out in the wilds, surrounded by trees and bushes, and without even a compass to tell him the way, Francis almost panicked. But he knew that if he once gave way to panic, he would be lost indeed. He had heard stories of men being lost in the bush, and going mad in the effort to find a way out. The only thing to do, he knew, was to keep his head and to refuse to give way to fright.

It was getting dark. He had a blanket with him. So he calmly unpacked the blanket, found a small hollow in the ground, and lay down there to sleep. The next morning he was still no closer to knowing where he was. But he remembered crossing a small stream, and he tried to work out his position from the sun, since he knew the part of the sky in which it had risen. In the end he found his little stream, but he knew now that he would never again venture into bush country without at least a compass with him.

When he reached the huts which had been put up to house the gold-seekers, he found that his chance of making a fortune was small. People had got there before him, and had staked claims for miles around. He managed to pick up one or two pieces of rock which had specks of gold in them; but the specks were so small that it was necessary to use a magnifying glass to see them! He was disappointed that he was not, after all, to be one of the pioneers in a new gold-field. But all the same, the adventure had been worth while, even though it had nearly ended in tragedy when he had got lost.

So back he tramped to the saw-mill and the railway. He was not taken back, but was given the sack because he had left his job without permission. So here he was, with very little money and no job. Pack on back again, he set out to find some new work.

Francis was not afraid of work, though in a way he valued adventure more. But now he had something quite different. He got a job at a coal-mine. It was very different from the coal-mines of Britain, of which he knew a little. There were no cages going down deep shafts. The men had to climb up a steep mountain, and then enter through a tunnel which had been dug into the mountainside. The coal itself was very soft, and when some of it had been dug out it crumbled, and the hands of the men looked as if they had been dipped into powdered lead.

There were, too, props to be fitted up at intervals, to prevent the top of the tunnel falling in, and one of Francis's first jobs at the coal-mine was to fit a series of props into a tunnel the wall of which had been damaged by an accident. This was as hard a task as he had ever tackled, for the props were fourteen feet long, and they took a lot of handling.

The timber was often damp, too, which meant that the props slipped about when they were handled, and they were very difficult to fit into position. Five men were generally occupied in lifting the props, and to get five men to work in unison on such a task was not at all easy. Many times people were injured, attempting this job more or less in darkness. One man had his back injured, and was away from work for months. Another man suffered a broken leg. Francis was lucky, he thought, in that the only injury that came his way in this time was a squashed finger.

Francis soon became known as a man who could handle horses. The coal was brought out of the tunnel in trucks, pulled by ponies. So he was now often in charge of the ponies, which pulled a row of trucks (called a "race" by the miners) along the tunnel and out into the open air.

Unlike most of his comrades, however, Francis could look ahead. He was now twenty years of age, and was earning quite good money. But he was completely dependent on what he was earning. He liked an adventurous life, but he could see that there was no future in this coal-mine. He might work there for twenty years, and still be no different from what he was at his present age. And, as he got older, he would not be as strong. He would find himself less and less able to go on with the hard grind in the mine. He told himself that it would soon be time to look for something with better prospects and a chance of making a bit more cash.

When he had left home and had set sail for New Zealand, he had made up his mind that he would not come back until he had saved £20,000. There was certainly nothing like this sum of money to be made in coal-mining. And a new effort at gold-hunting in the bush soon showed him that there were very few people making big money in this either. So what should he do?

For a short time he went from door to door selling yearly subscriptions to a weekly paper. The owner of the paper had promised to pay him his expenses, plus a commission on the number of subscriptions that he succeeded in selling. He was very successful at this. When the owners of the paper found that his commission alone would amount to about £8 a week, they queried much of the expenses that he had spent, mainly in travelling. He was not prepared to go on with a job where his employers did not trust him, so he gave up that job, though he might have been earning £400 a year—a big advance on anything that he had previously been making.

He had now come to the conclusion that there was more money to be made in selling things than there was in the slogging hard work of mining. For a time he worked for a firm who were marketing a book-keeping system to farmers. Most New Zealand farmers in those days found it very difficult to keep accounts which the Income Tax authorities could understand, and so they were often forced to pay a lot more Income Tax than they really should have done. This system of book-keeping was designed to help them in this problem. Here again Francis was successful, and he managed to persuade a number of farmers to adopt the new system of book-keeping.

He found that if he visited five farms each day, he could usually succeed in selling the system to at least two of them. That was a pretty high proportion of sales, and he told himself that if he could stick at this job for a year he would have saved quite a lot of money. This was one path to a small fortune, if not to the £20,000 that he had originally set as his target.

This job involved a lot of travelling, so he bought himself a motor-bicycle to get around the country. It was the first machine of any sort that he had ever owned, and it met a very real need. It made, too, a pleasant change from all the horse-riding that he had been doing.

It was not what a young man forty years later would have thought much good. It could be started only by running with it along the road, and then, when the engine started, leaping into the saddle before the machine ran away. If the engine stalled when being driven up a hill, he had to push it painfully to the top. Then he had to start it by running it down the other side and jumping on when the engine began to fire.

After a few months of this, he began to get very tired of the pushing and running, so he sold it and bought an old Ford car. He had a push-bike, too. He used to set off for a new district in the car, carrying the push-bike with him. A tent also was part of his regular luggage. Then, when he had reached a suitable spot, he would park the car just off the road, pitch his tent alongside it, and use the push-bike to get to the farms, which were often well away from the road. The rough tracks leading to the farm-houses were usually quite unsuitable for driving a car, but a bicycle could negotiate them without too much difficulty.

He found that he could keep up his sales to two farmers out of every five he visited, and he reckoned that if this could be maintained, he would be earning good money, and would be thought satisfactory by his employers.

He was, in this way, gradually working his way across New Zealand. This was just the sort of life that he liked, giving him new scenes to look at week by week. He saw much of the scenery of the dominion, and got much pleasure out of this wandering life.

He made friends, too. There was one man whom he got to know well. This man had invented a folding canvas canoe, in which Francis sometimes went sailing with him. On one occasion they were mistaken for one of the competitors in a sailing race. This was the first time that Francis had come into contact with such events.

When he had done his year of selling the book-keeping scheme, he had earned about £700, and had saved £400 of it. This was not bad, and he felt fairly happy. Few young men of twenty-one had as much business ability in those days, and the value of money was much greater, of course, than it was to be in the years ahead.

However, Francis had set himself the task of working for one year in this job, and the year was now up. He was now offered a post with a firm of land agents, who were making money by buying and selling houses and land. He had to invest most of his savings into the firm, but when he had studied the firm's books, he thought that it would be a good investment. So Goodwin and Chichester, land agents, came into existence. Francis had, of course, little direct knowledge of how houses were built. But he was a lively man, and was soon capable of mastering even a completely strange business.

He got married, too. But this proved to be a disaster. It was partly that his wife was a purely domestic person, with no interest outside the home, while Francis led an extremely active life in the outside world. They had a son, called George. But soon his wife went off to live with her own relatives, and Francis, realising that this marriage was hopelessly unhappy, continued to live by himself in Wellington.

He found city life quite congenial. It certainly made a change after the long months that he had spent out in the wilds. Sitting in an office sometimes seemed a little dull to the adventurous young man. But there was a fair amount of travel, and this added variety to what might otherwise have been a fairly tame kind of life for Francis Chichester.

His fortune was piling up, too. The firm prospered, for in those days Wellington was a growing city, which meant that those who were dealing in land and houses found an ever-increasing demand for the things that they had to sell.

Goodwin, Francis's partner, had an agency for a large insurance concern, and this brought in a fairly large extra income.

So all seemed set fair. All Francis's friends felt that he was settling down to be a business man, and anyone who had known him would have said that his old wanderlust and love for adventure had disappeared. But it was not so.

CHAPTER THREE

FLYING

FRANCIS CHICHESTER would have been amazed in those days if he had been told that a development of the land agent's business was to lead him to one of the main strands of his life. So it was to be. And it happened in this way.

Goodwin and Chichester were making good money, true. But Francis thought that they were wasting a lot of time over the agency business which they were handling—both the insurance agency and the handling of property on behalf of various owners, collecting rents, supervising repairs, and so on. He considered that, now that they had a good balance in the bank, they should concentrate on handling their own property.

"You think we can afford to give up the agency business?" Goodwin asked him one day, when they had been discussing this new idea.

"I'm sure of it."

"You don't think we'd drop a lot of money?"

Chichester grinned happily. "If we owned more property of our own, we should be working for ourselves and not for other people," he said. "That is the way that we can make more money, and not less."

In the end he had his way. They started buying pieces of land and other property on the outskirts of the city of Wellington. Sometimes they would sell the land off for building. Sometimes, if they thought it was an area where building would spoil the general appearance of the district, they would sell it for some other use. There was one fifty-acre piece of land, for instance, which they bought at an auction sale, and then divided it into plots for allotment gardens. They built a road through the property, and the allotments were in great demand. This showed them what could be done by buying with care and knowing exactly what they were doing with the property that they bought.

But for a time they went carefully, not plunging too deeply or buying anything very big. They thought that they would have to play for safety and feel their way, until they had enough experience to know just what could be done without taking an undue risk. They had some money behind them, but they could not take any chance of losing this.

Then one day a large piece of land came on the market. This was at a place called Silverstream, some ten miles from Wellington. It was the biggest thing that they had ever considered buying. Over 1,000 acres in extent, it meant that they would be sinking an awful lot of money in the purchase. There were long and anxious talks before they finally decided that this was too good a chance to miss, and soon they found themselves the owners of 1,000 acres of land. It was in some ways an almost frightening thought. But Francis was sure that this was something that would put them both on the road to fortune.

The land, of course, could not be left as it was. It had to be developed in some way, if it was ever to make money. Again there were anxious consultations before they came to a decision as to just what they were to do with it.

They realised that this might be a long-term investment. They might have to wait years before some of their money came back. But they were both young men; they were neither of them hard-up for cash. So if they could think of something that would bring in money years ahead, this would be worth doing.

"Trees!" Geoffrey Goodwin exclaimed one day.

"Trees?" Francis Chichester was puzzled.

"Yes, trees. Some of those pine-trees grow quickly. How would it be if we planted pine-trees on part of the land at Silverstream? There will be a huge demand for timber in this country for many years to come. If we can wait a few years, we shall get a good return for our money."

This seemed a very sensible argument, and Francis agreed quite willingly. Soon they set about this great task of getting a large number of baby pine-trees. These were destined to grow and then to be cut down, bringing in a considerable income for their owners. They decided that the cheapest way of getting the trees was to collect seed from the pine-cones which lay about in large quantities. Properly planted and tended, these seeds would sprout and produce small trees, which could then be spaced out on the part of the land which they thought most suitable. Francis took charge of the seed-planting job. Many thousands of the seeds had to be planted, and this took quite a time.

Soon the seeds sprouted, and the little seedling trees emerged. These had to be transplanted separately. They tried out a few at first, to be sure that they had been using the right methods. They had to leave enough space to allow the trees to grow in the years ahead. They allowed nine feet between the trees, and six feet between the rows in which they were planted.

The first batch soon settled in, and began to grow quite healthily. So they decided to go ahead on a large scale. This meant that they had to recruit some men to work for them. They found that the trees put on an inch in diameter each year, and grew every year something like six feet in height. As it turned out, it was Geoffrey Goodwin's son, some years later, who started cutting the trees and sending them to the sawmill for turning into planks. Francis Chichester can claim to be one of the few men who have planted a forest and seen its trees turned into timber in his own lifetime.

This took a lot of money. Some they raised by selling off plots of land to people who wanted weekend cottages in the country. They extended their interests in all sorts of directions. They bought a company making chairs for cinemas and theatres. Everything they touched seemed to prosper. Gone were the days when Francis Chichester calculated his income in a few pounds a week. By the time he reached his twenty-sixth birthday he was earning many thousands of pounds a year.

And then—a real turning-point in his life, though he did not see it at the time—the Goodwin-Chichester Aviation Company was founded.

This was intended mainly as a money-making concern, giving people pleasure flights at a time when few people had been up in an aeroplane. They were granted the agency in New Zealand from the English company of A. V. Roe, bought two aeroplanes from them, and signed up four pilots who had experience in flying during the war, mostly with machines a good deal heavier than the Avro Avians which Goodwin and Chichester had bought.

Ever since those far-off days in Upavon, Francis had been fascinated by flying, and now he got wildly excited

at the thought that he was part-owner of two aeroplanes.
Then he had the thought—why should he not learn to
fly himself? He was a good car-driver, and had mechanical
sense. Flying an aeroplane, he told himself, would not be
all that different from driving a car. They had suffered a
number of crashes with their flights—mainly because the
pilots sometimes had to land in small fields—and Francis
thought that if he could handle an aeroplane himself he
might be able to suggest ways of avoiding these expensive
accidents. And, apart from this, it would be a good thing
to be able to act as substitute for one of their pilots, if
illness should prevent the pilot from taking his machine
into the air. He was keen to learn how to fly, anyway, and
all this reinforced his decision.

So he went to one of the New Zealand Air Force
Stations. It was near the city of Christchurch. Here he
had his first flying lessons. He found that there were many
difficulties which he had not expected. There was no
proper throttle on the engine in those days. When a pilot
wished to land he had to switch the engine off and coast
in, keeping a careful eye on the ground so that he made a
smooth landing and avoided collisions with trees and
hedges.

Also the engine spouted oil, which sometimes splashed
back into the pilot's face. This was a very unpleasant
affair. For a long time Francis found the experience of
flying, while exciting, by no means as delightful as he had
thought that it was likely to be.

He was given lessons, as was necessary with a beginner,
in a dual-control machine, which could be controlled
either by him, as the learner, or by the experienced pilot
who was teaching him. By the end of 1928 he had done
some eighteen hours in the air, but still was not good

enough to be trusted in the air with a machine on his own. Naturally, the flying part of his life was only part of his activities. He was a business man first and a pilot second, and to learn to master a complicated thing like an aeroplane is really a full-time job.

In 1929 he went back to England for the first time in ten years. He had the idea that he would fly back to New Zealand. This would in a way be cheaper, and he would be delivering another machine to be put into service with his company. He knew, however, that as he was still not an experienced pilot he would have to get a very reliable machine. He would also have to have more flying lessons in England, so as to improve his very poor performances at Christchurch.

He tried out all sorts of machines, and found few of them completely satisfactory. He had lessons at Brook-lands, the motor-racing centre which at that time was also used as a flying field. In August he flew solo for the first time, though only for five minutes. A week or two later he was granted his pilot's licence. This was some-thing of an achievement, for he had flown only about twenty-four hours in the dual-control machines, and only six or seven hours of this instruction had taken place in England.

In September he bought the aeroplane. It was a Gipsy Moth—a name which was to be associated with Francis Chichester in many ways for many years. The first day he took it to Liverpool, where a friend of his was appearing at a theatre. Finding difficulty in getting to the airfield, he turned around and flew down to North Devon, to visit his parents. It was a wonderful thought, that he could speed across, from one end of England to another like this. But the aeroplane had no compass, and he could make out his route only by following the main railway lines.

He found it difficult to get on with his family. He had been away so long, and now spoke with an unfamiliar New Zealand accent. He thought that he had done pretty well to have left England with £10 and come back worth £20,000. But this thought did not appear to enter his father's head. Francis took friends and relatives for small flights, had one or two minor crashes, and then, one day, took up an old man who had formerly been their family gardener. This was on his twenty-eighth birthday, and the gardener recalled that it was on that day, twenty-eight years before, that he had ridden into Barnstaple, to fetch the doctor who was to attend Mrs. Chichester on the occasion of Francis's birth.

Francis was delighted to be flying his own machine, though he knew that he was, as yet, by no means a skilled pilot. He knew that he would have to have much more experience before he could undertake a long-distance flight. On coming back from North Devon he landed at Brooklands in a wind. This tipped the aeroplane almost on its side. One wing touched the ground and crumpled up. Francis was appalled when he got out and examined the damage. However, he thought that he could put it right himself. He set to with a will on these repairs. The staff of the airfield was astonished to see a pilot doing running repairs to his own machine.

When it was in good condition again, he set about proper training. He practised landing on different kinds of surfaces, in winds and in rain. He knew that if he was to attempt any long flight he would have to know a lot more about handling the machine than he had yet learned.

It was well into October before a compass arrived, which had to be fitted on the new machine. This gave

Francis more confidence. Soon after he took off at night, flew for some twenty-five miles in moonlight, and landed without any mishap. This was one of the most delightful things that had ever happened to him, and it went a long way towards encouraging him to go on with his schemes for undertaking a flight across the world.

His idea now was to fly solo from England to Australia. Only once before had that been done, and this by a crack test pilot with hundreds of hours of flying experience. Chichester thought he would have to give himself some months before he could undertake such a hazardous adventure. One of his problems was money. The business in New Zealand was still working at a profit, and he had a good share in it, so he cabled to Geoffrey Goodwin and asked him to send over £400. Then he decided that, before starting on such a journey as that to Australia, he would have a run around Europe.

Here he found another difficulty. Insurance companies were very reluctant to insure him; but in the end he found a company prepared to do this, if he would undertake to have with him to cross the English Channel a pilot with longer experience than his own. He met a man called Joe King, a pilot of long experience, and persuaded him to come on the trip. This was just a flight undertaken for fun; but Francis thought that it would give him experience and confidence before he started on that much longer and more dangerous flight to Australia.

He set off for his grand tour of Europe in November— by no means the best time of the year for flying. When they started, they cleared the trees at the end of the airfield only by a couple of feet. Francis thought that Joe King wanted to take charge, so he did not touch the controls. After they had missed the trees so narrowly, they found that neither of them had touched the levers at all—the machine had virtually got itself into the air!

The next few days were very exciting. Paris, Nice, Milan, Venice and down into Jugoslavia. Francis saw countries which had previously been only names in the geography books. All the time, too, he was learning more about how to control an aeroplane, how to navigate, how to keep the compass in view and to fly blind through clouds and storms. It was all very fine experience, which was to be of the greatest possible value to him in the days ahead.

He landed in a field in Jugoslavia, and was taken to be a Russian spy. However, he found a man who spoke French, and to him he was able to explain just who he was and what he was doing. He had left Joe King in Paris, and a good deal of the flying in Southern Europe was solo work, which brought many anxious moments. Especially difficult, he found, was estimating time, with the result that sometimes he had to land in the dark in totally unfamiliar country.

He reached Warsaw, where he was entertained by important officials. But, quite apart from the problems of actually flying the machine, there were the additional matters of arguments with customs officials, who thought he might be smuggling.

Back he came across Germany. Finally he flew solo across the English Channel, only about fifty feet above the water.

It had been an exciting and on the whole enjoyable journey. And at the end of it Francis Chichester knew that he was a genuine pilot.

It was on November 20 that he arrived back in England. He felt now that he was fairly well able to face the long and onerous journey to Australia. He knew that what he had done in his trip around Europe would be child's play compared to the flight across the world. But he had extra confidence in himself and his ability. He had got the "feel" of the machine. He knew exactly what it would do, and what he himself could do with it.

Francis was never put off by danger. He was well aware that there was danger in undertaking a journey such as only one man had done before. But this was the real sort of adventure at which he had all his life been aiming.

There were all sorts of preparations to be made. His New Zealand partner had sent him the four hundred pounds requested, but the European journey had eaten up half of this. He would, before flying to Australia, have to get permission to land in many countries, some of them with governments that were a trifle suspicious of what Great Britain was up to, and might suspect him of being a spy. He got a cable from Geoffrey Goodwin advising him to sell the machine, as repairs in Malaya (which was to be one of his ports of call) were very expensive. Solo flights of any distance at that time were almost unknown, and there was always the possibility of having to make a crash landing somewhere, in which case the cost would be terrific.

One of the petrol companies promised to lay on petrol supplies for the whole journey at a cheap price. But in order that this could be arranged, he would have to let them know in advance exactly where he planned to land for refuelling.

Bert Hinkler, the famous test pilot who up to that time had made the only solo flight from England to Australia, had done the journey in fifteen and a half days. This meant a daily journey of about 750 miles. Francis was now consumed with a new ambition. This was to beat Hinkler's record. He felt fairly sure that he could manage this, though he knew only too well that it would be by no means easy to do so.

Francis studied maps and worked out routes. He did not want to beat Hinkler by a few minutes only. He divided his journey into 500-mile stages, and made up his mind that, if at all possible, he would do two of these stages in each day, with a brief rest in between. The distance, all told, was about 12,000 miles, and that would mean that he would do it in twelve days. This was if he had no serious mishaps and was able to stick to the schedule that he had worked out.

Another snag was that the Gipsy Moth had no navigation lights, as it was not designed for night flying. Yet, if he was to carry out his plans, he would have to do a fair amount of night flying. The only navigation lights available were meant for much bigger and heavier machines. The Gipsy Moth could not possibly be fitted with them, as they would add too much weight to the little machine.

So off Francis went to the Air Ministry. Would it be possible, he wanted to know, to get permission to fly in the dark over certain countries, without showing any navigation lights? He did not want to risk being shot down by some suspicious policeman on an airfield in some distant country.

Officials at the Air Ministry were dubious about all this. In the end, though, they managed to get the necessary permission. But there were still other things to be done. He would have mainly to eat while flying. So he had to alter the cockpit so that food could be stored at a spot easy to get at, without having to cease his grip on the control levers. He also had to make other alterations, so that a rubber boat, which he carried as a precautionary measure, would be easy to get out, if he were unlucky enough to have to make a forced landing in the sea.

The hazard of flying solo over wide stretches of sea was, indeed, probably the greatest danger that he would have to face. Crash-landing on the sea would be a desperate gamble. And that was something the possibility of which Francis knew he would have to face.

He had no illusions about the risks involved in this long journey of many thousands of miles. He faced all these, and knew that he was taking a chance, risking his life a hundred times. But all the same that journey around Europe had given him a lot of confidence in his own skill. He was sure that he could do the journey, and knock days off the record that Bert Hinkler had set up.

Geoffrey Goodwin in New Zealand was probably by this time more anxious about Francis than Francis was about himself. Francis had so much to arrange, so many problems to get over, that he had little time to worry about the details of the actual flight itself. Geoffrey, when he cabled about the problems of possible repairs in Malaya, knew that there were many other possible snags that might have to be overcome.

Francis was not worried, however, and was very excited. The aeroplane was still at Brooklands, and the first little flight was to the big airport at Croydon, where there were customs sheds and all the other necessary offices for dealing with a man taking off for a long flight.

It was on December 19 that this little hop took place. As he taxied along the runway at Brooklands, Francis drew a deep breath. His first big adventure had started!

CHAPTER FOUR

OFF TO AUSTRALIA

ODDLY enough, his first difficulty came almost at once. When he landed at Croydon, where he was to clear matters with the customs officials, he was at once stopped and asked why he had no navigation lights on his machine. He managed to explain this and to get all the necessary documents for his journey. Soon he was on his way.

As he ran the machine for its take-off he had a moment of panic. This was the first time that he had tried to fly it with a full load, for now he had to carry food, as well as more fuel than he had ever before taken with him. It was in the middle of the night, and he found steering his course difficult to begin with. He found himself over the English Channel, but had not calculated his distances properly. Still, he was soon flying across France, and in the end landed at Lyons after seven hours in the air.

The machine swung to one side at the Lyons airfield. Luckily, no damage was done. Francis recalled that the take-off from Croydon had been bumpy, and now, as he climbed down from the cockpit, he saw the reason. One tyre was burst! This also explained the reason for the swing on landing. However, the tyre was soon mended, and he was off again on his second hop for that day. Pisa, in Italy, was his target for that night.

As he came near, he thought he could see the airfield, with a huge searchlight illuminating the sky. He thought it was good of the authorities to have put this on for him, but as he dropped lower he suddenly realized that he was not, after all, aiming for the airfield. The "searchlight" was the headlamp of a car. He was very nearly landing in the middle of the city. He swept up into the air again, and found the airfield not far away. It was in complete darkness, with even the runways not lit.

He landed without any incidents, except that the wheels of the plane got stuck in thick mud. A group of soldiers appeared and pushed it out of this. Chichester asked why there were no lights to assist him in landing, and they said that they had thought he would circle around overhead for some time, and were arranging to have the lights switched on in good time for him. But, owing to the fact that he had landed so quickly, he had beaten them to it.

He had done 750 miles that day, but this was short of his calculated average of about 1,000 miles per day. He therefore went to bed at 10 that night, got up again before two in the morning, and set off again. There were still no lights on the airport, so, as he said, he had spent a night at an airport which he never saw.

Also he had not really had enough sleep. As he flew on over Italy, he got sleepier and sleepier, having to jump up and down in his seat and swing his arms about to keep himself awake. He landed at Catania, where he had again to go through all the formalities of the customs. He also took on petrol. He slept for about a quarter of an hour there, which did him some good. It gave him confidence for the flight across the Mediterranean, towards Africa.

He had resolved to reach Africa in two days from Croydon. Otherwise he might have spent the night in Malta. He reached the African continent; but by now it was getting dark again. He had planned to land at a place called Homs, but was unable to see either the town or the airfield. Rapidly looking at a map, he decided that his best bet was to push along the coast to Tripoli. where he knew that the Italian Air Force had a base.

Once again he had the deceptive appearance of a searchlight. He thought he was near the airfield. It appeared that the searchlight was being switched on and off at regular intervals of time. He took this as being an effort to signal to him by the airfield staff.

As he came lower, however, he saw that this time the "searchlight" was actually a lighthouse, marking the entrance to the harbour! He had nearly crash-landed in water. Circling around, he hunted the dark horizon for some hint that he was near the Italian airfield, but for a time he could not see it. He thought he could see another light flashing, several miles away. When he got close to it, he discovered that it was a car, flashing its headlights to indicate that it wanted to pass another, slower-moving vehicle. Still, no airfield to be seen.

Finally, he thought he had spotted it. He came down, sure that he was in the right place. Suddenly there was a crash, and the Gipsy Moth tipped up. Chichester was thrown forward. He groaned. A crash-landing, he thought. This was the end of his ambition to fly from England to Australia.

He scrambled out of the machine, and found his feet in water. Had he, by some mischance, landed in the sea? Then he realised that he was not sinking in. The water was only a few inches deep. He had landed in a kind of shallow, flat pond.

Soon some soldiers arrived. He had found the airfield, but had been unlucky to land in this water which was nearby.

By this time Chichester was too sleepy to want anything but a bed. An Italian officer gave him a glass of wine, which he drank gratefully. Then he was taken away to a bedroom, and was asleep almost as soon as his head touched the pillow.

Next morning the soldiers pushed the aeroplane in. It was not as badly damaged as Chichester had feared. The propeller was damaged and one wing-strut was broken, but that was all, in spite of the machine having pitched forward on its nose.

Now Chichester could look back at what he had already done. In forty hours from leaving England, his actual time in the air had been twenty-six hours, and in that time he had travelled nearly two thousand miles. His average was all right up to date. But what about the damage to his machine? It was not the complete "write-off" that he had feared on landing. But how long would the repairs take?

A new propeller would have to be brought out from England. That was the real snag. And in those days spare parts for aeroplanes were much more difficult to get than spare parts for cars. Chichester got on the long-distance telephone to the makers. They said that they could rush out a new propeller for him as quickly as possible, but that it was unlikely that it would reach him for nine or ten days. So there was no chance, now, of beating the England to Australia record, though it might be possible to beat the record, in terms of actual hours spent in the air.

The ten days spent there were not unpleasant, though Chichester felt annoyed and frustrated that a mishap of this sort should ruin his great ambition to set a new record time for this journey across the world. The Italians tried to make him feel at home, provided good food and a comfortable bed. He could do nothing but sit back and wait for the new propeller to arrive.

The airfield engineers repaired the broken wing-strut, and Chichester was charged nothing for this.

When in the end the machine was again airworthy, Chichester was a little nervous. He knew now that he had overdone things on those two tremendous days from Croydon to Tripoli, and he had made up his mind not to attempt to push along so quickly again. But there had been a number of crashes to Italian machines during the ten days he had spent at Tripoli, and he wondered if flying over Africa was an unhealthy occupation.

Still, with whatever misgivings, he took off. Africa looked very beautiful there, underneath him. He wondered if the repairs had been properly done, and if the new propeller would be as good as the one which it replaced. He tried some stunts and aerobatics, to see if the machine was responding to the controls as it used to do. On the whole it succeeded, though there were some very anxious moments, when he felt that the Gipsy Moth was not doing what it should have done.

There were problems of weather too. He struck a sandstorm at one point over the desert. The air looked like mud. He could see nothing, and he wondered what would happen did he run into this sort of weather after dark. Still, he soon flew out of the cloud of sand, and into brilliant sunshine. At the end of eight hours he had done nearly 600 miles, and landed at Benghazi. Here he had an interesting hour, but felt some uneasiness when told that only a day or two before the Italians had been bombing some rebellious Arabs, only about ten miles away. How would the Arabs look at him, a European, if he had to make a forced landing in what they thought of as their territory? It was yet another danger to be added to all the dangers he had already thought about.

A message arrived while he was there, telling him that his wife had died in New Zealand. This was a shock, though they had not seen much of each other in recent months.

He had eaten food at intervals while flying—dates, cheese, biscuits, sardines and tinned fruit. But as he flew on he got more and more tired and stiff, and was not able to eat anything more. He had not, when planning this flight, thought of the tiredness from which he was bound to suffer, nor had he thought that the cramped conditions of the cockpit would make him shuffle about, trying to get into a more comfortable position—usually in vain.

He had meant to land at Mersa Matruh, to clear the customs. But when he did a calculation, thinking of distance and time, he thought that he would be wise to fly farther on, before darkness descended. In the end, when he did land, there was yet another message waiting for him. This ordered him to fly back to Cairo, to go through the necessary formalities with the customs. He had to sign a form at once saying that he had received this message.

He decided to risk ignoring the message. So he took off again, and headed towards Palestine. He landed at Gaza to refuel, and found that one of the cylinders of the engine was not working properly. A valve needed attention. It would have to be dealt with pretty soon.

He then landed, after a further flight of some hours, at a place called Rutbah, and here he was fortunate enough to find a mechanic, employed by the British firm of Imperial Airways. This man agreed to try to deal with the defective cylinder. So that was one worry the less.

Francis slept well that night. But it was bitterly cold, and the next morning he had a terribly difficult job getting the engine started. The oil, he thought, was probably frozen.

Baghdad was the next stop. Here customs, refuelling, everything was ready, and so there was little waste of time. He was on the ground for less than an hour getting everything done. By now Chichester had almost lost count of the number of countries he had visited since leaving Croydon. His next stop was in Persia, at a town called Bushire. Here he slept on a camp-bed. He had meant to get up early the next morning, and at five o'clock he landed on the floor with a bang. The camp-bed had split!

On and on he flew. By now the journey was getting almost monotonous, and Chichester realised something that he was again to have brought home to him in the future. This was the intense loneliness of a man doing a long journey without any human company. The breaks, when he came down to refuel, were welcome, too, because he had some talk with staff at the various airfields. On the way to Karachi he got bored, but his boredom was relieved by seeing a large school of porpoises playing in the sea.

The journey across India took several days. Four times he refuelled in these days. One night he slept at Jhansi, where he found some R.A.F. pilots who were on exercises. They turned up in force to make him welcome, supplied him with a camp-bed which this time did not split, and even a canvas bath, which was very welcome and refreshing.

The engine was now making rough, rattling noises, and Chichester wondered if there was something seriously wrong with it. After all, he had been pushing that engine fairly hard for some days now, and there was no knowing if it did not need careful checking and servicing.

It turned out to be the valves of the cylinder which had previously given trouble, which were still not working effectively. At Calcutta he found a mechanic, working for a company doing air surveys, and this man reground the valves for him. The nasty noises in the engine now grew much less, and Chichester felt a good deal happier about it.

He was now getting tired again. This was because, after his long hours in the air, he found the long conversations during his short periods on the ground getting tiresome. When he took off, he found himself feeling wearier and wearier. There were, in fact, all sorts of problems which had never entered his head when he was planning the flight in far-off England.

Somehow, though, he managed to push on. In Singapore he had a cheerful evening with a group of R.A.F. officers who were in charge of flying-boats, based on the harbour there. Then down across the Pacific to the Dutch island of Sumatra. Here the sun was so hot that, as he came into land, it was burning the side of his neck most painfully. And there was nowhere, it seemed, suitable to land. There were black storm-clouds in the sky, and visibility was very poor. He tried to land where he thought there was a gap in the clouds, and found himself diving straight into the sea! He just managed to get the Gipsy Moth flying upward again. Sumatra was useless, for his purposes. He had some fuel still available, so he decided to fly on to the sister island of Java.

Here weather conditions were far better. There was a very modern and well-equipped airport. And Francis

Chichester himself has recorded that when he came down he was surprised to be surrounded by a crowd of handsome Dutchmen, all of them speaking perfect English.

He stayed on Java for a day. It was enjoyable but tiring, as there were hosts of people who wanted to talk to him. His dramatic flight across the world was now getting space in the newspapers of all countries. For the first time Chichester came to know what it was like to be a famous man, to whom everyone wanted to talk.

But there were various things that he wanted to discuss, and it seemed to him to be advisable to stay on for a day, in order to get these matters settled. For one thing, he wanted to land on the Dutch island of Timor—his last stopping-place before setting off on his last hop to Australia. He was not at all sure if there was a suitable landing-ground on Timor, and he thought that the authorities in Java might be able to give him some information on this point.

He had conflicting reports about this. One Dutch pilot he met in Java told him that there was an excellent airfield at a place called Koepang. Another said that this could not be used. And the man who said this was a Dutch air force pilot, who would be expected to know something of the Dutch government's feeling about such matters.

Maps, too, were unreliable. He studied a number of maps, but they did not appear to agree, even on distances. And with the fact that the Gipsy Moth would only take a limited amount of petrol, he had to know precisely the distances that he would need to fly between fuelling points.

There were no large-scale maps, as far as he could see. He could not get sight of any with a scale better than sixty-four miles to an inch. A map of that kind could not give much detail.

He did get off in the end, but still with some anxious thoughts in his mind. These were not improved by the fact that he now struck some bad weather, with heavy clouds and torrential rain, which made visibility almost nil. Yet there was nothing that he could do about this. He just had to push on and hope for the best. At one point the rain was so heavy that he turned back, trying to make for a spot where the weather had been clear. When he got there he found that the rain in front of him was even worse than that which he had left behind.

He was circling around, wondering what to do, when he spotted another aeroplane. This was a big Dutch machine, which was flying only a few feet from the surface of the sea. Perhaps, Chichester told himself, visibility was better down there. It was worth trying anyway.

He tried. At one point, peering through the rain, he spotted a small fishing-boat. This was only just ahead of him, and he pulled up quickly to a higher altitude. But he missed the masts of the boat by what seemed to be only a few inches. He breathed again. That had been the narrowest squeak yet. At another place he flew between the masts of a junk on the beach and another one a short distance out to sea. There were a number of Malayans on that beach, and they rushed away in great alarm as this strange machine seemed to roar at them from the sky.

He soon found a place where it seemed possible to land. Land he did. He found that the surface of the ground was soft, but the landing was quite satisfactory for all that.

This was a fairly primitive airfield, but it was an airfield of sorts, after all. Chichester had taken the precaution of writing down a few phrases in the Malayan language, and, by combining these with signs, he was able to tell a policeman who appeared that he wanted a guard put on his machine, and—above all—that he wanted to sleep.

This long period of flying almost blind through rainstorms had been the most tiring period yet. But he was beginning to feel that he was now within striking distance of his destination. He was, after all, well down in the Pacific. Australia was now not so far away, and he might hope to get there in a comparatively short time.

He calculated that he had taken nearly an hour and a half to do less than sixty miles—the slowest and shortest lap of the whole long journey up to this time. So bad had the weather been that this loss of time was something that had been quite impossible to avoid.

These parts, too, were sometimes full of savages—or people who looked like savages. At one island most of the men wore fearsome-looking knives in their belts. Here Chichester was asked, before he took off, to pay for the guard duty which had been carried out by twenty men who had surrounded his machine all night, while its owner slept.

After these adventures he reached Timor. As he came down to the airfield the place felt like a furnace. The heat was almost unbearable.

Ahead, too, was the longest sea-crossing of the whole journey, and Francis Chichester decided that the engine wanted careful checking. To come down on land in an emergency might be difficult; but to come down in the sea would mean the end of everything. So before starting he had to be as certain as he possibly could that the engine was in perfect working order.

This job took five hours, part of them hours of darkness.

A Dutch officer had lent Chichester some oil lamps, but these attracted thousands of flying insects, and as he worked on the engine he found that flying ants were landing on his eyes and ears. They were very difficult to get rid of, and he took much longer over the job than he would have done without this handicap.

He took all possible precautions. He blew up the rubber boat which had been his insurance against a forced landing in the sea. Then he tied a rope to it, so that, if he did crash in the sea, he could swiftly pull it out, and so escape from death by drowning.

By this time he had faced so many dangers that the danger of the Timor Sea did not appear as frightening as it might have done a week or two before. Yet this was no reason for not taking all possible measures to ensure his safety in the event of some sudden emergency.

The actual water crossing, as far as he could calculate it from his maps, would be about 320 miles. That may not appear very far; but he might crash into the sea far from the routes of shipping. He might have to stay afloat for hours, or even days, if the worst came to the worst. Chichester was never a pessimist; but he liked to be prepared for anything which might happen.

He had aimed at a spot north of Darwin as his target on the Australian coast. The sea crossing, the most hazardous part of the journey, was almost dull. There were no difficulties, and the Gipsy Moth flew like a bird. The journey from Timor to Darwin was about 500 miles long, and he did it in a little over six hours.

He was in Australia! He thought that there might be a number of people to meet him, but when he landed at Darwin airport he attracted little attention. A few people glanced at him almost without curiosity, though he had made what was really one of the great epic flights of the century.

In the end he was met by an agent of the oil company which had supplied him with his fuel throughout the journey. He took this man and one or two others to a nearby hotel for a glass of beer. So quietly did the main part of his journey end—it might have been just a journey from London to Brighton or from Manchester to Blackpool, instead of Croydon to Darwin. But it will always remain one of the great adventure stories in the early history of aviation.

CHAPTER FIVE

FLYING ON !

THE last little bit of this flight was something of an anti-climax, after all the excitements of the Timor Sea. A night in Darwin, quite enjoyable, and then soon moving deeper into Australia; that was Chichester's programme.

To begin with, he followed something of the same method as he had followed in Britain in his first flight in a Gipsy Moth. That is to say, he followed railway lines, which he had studied on maps, so that he knew just where they were going to lead him. And if the railway line ended, there was usually a telegraph line instead, which he could see quite well, a kind of spider's web, spun over the wild countryside.

In this manner, he made his way into the interior of Australia. There were many difficult spots, in northern Australia especially, in that places marked on the maps as towns turned out to be tiny villages. Refuelling was difficult in such conditions. It was, in some respects, the most difficult part of the whole journey. For one thing, there were, when he had lost both the railway lines and the telegraph lines, no landmarks which would help him to know just where he was on the map.

To begin with, when he was well clear of Darwin, he headed for a town called Comooweal. The petrol gauge was now showing that he was almost completely out of fuel, and it was important to find a place where he could land and find petrol. He wrote, when describing this part of his journey, that he soon lost the desire to find that town of Comooweal—"if only I could see a building!"

In the end he felt compelled to land. He found a sign that human beings had lived and worked there at some time in the not too distant past. There were dismal sheds, made of empty petrol tins. But there were no full petrol tins, and there were no people anywhere to be seen.

Not far away he found a road. But there seemed to be no traffic at all on it. Not for the first time since leaving Croydon, he felt terribly isolated and alone. He had thought that when he arrived in Australia all his worries would be over and done with. But this appeared to be an over-optimistic way of looking at things.

The only water that he could find was thick with mud. He drank a little from a bottle of wine that he had brought from Italy, but it now tasted like poison.

Chichester was very worried indeed now. He did not know just where he was in the vast of Australia. He was aiming at getting to Melbourne or Sydney or one of the great cities of the Australian continent. How was he to find them? Would the newspapers soon be reporting his arrival at Darwin, only to say that he had left Darwin, never to be seen again?

He spent that night in the rubber boat from the Gipsy Moth. It provided something like an air-cushion on which to sleep. In spite of his worries, Chichester did not sleep at all badly. He always had the gift of being able to dismiss his worries, even if only for a short time.

The next morning he studied the district around. It was a bit muddy, and he could detect tracks of one sort and another. There were, at one spot, the marks of horses' hooves. And the horses had been shod ! That meant that he was not very far from some measure of civilisation.

Then he found what he took to be the marks of cart-wheels. This was better still, and he followed them for some distance. In the end, he found that they were the marks of the wheels of his own aeroplane!

He would have to fly on. That was beyond all question. But how much petrol had he got left? The petrol gauge showed "Empty"—but then, like so many petrol gauges on vehicles of many sorts, it was set to do this a little too soon, thus causing some alarm while there was still time.

He had a big tin, and he drained the petrol into this. About three gallons of petrol still remained in the tank. The Gipsy Moth, while fairly economical in petrol, did not do many miles to the gallon, and Chichester reckoned that the three gallons he now had left would take him for something over half an hour's flying. He could go twenty miles out and twenty miles back. This was allowing a little extra for the acceleration that would be needed for starting and taking off.

There was still a haze on the air, which made visibility very limited. Should he wait and see if this cleared? Or should he take off and cruise about, hoping to see Comoo-weal through the haze? The decision as to what to do was one of the most difficult and awkward that he had to make, all through this adventurous time of his life. But Francis Chichester was never a very patient man. He always wanted to push on with whatever was the task in hand. So it was that he now came to the conclusion that the best thing to do was to get moving. For one thing, he feared that if he had been reported missing, the Australian Air Force might search for him. And an organised search was the last thing that he wanted to have to endure.

He started the engine, gave it two or three minutes to warm up, and then took off. He was well aware that this was something of a gamble—perhaps the biggest gamble of his life, up to date. But at the same time he thought it to be a gamble that he could not well resist.

He decided to fly eastwards for about a quarter of an hour. If, by the end of that time, he had seen nothing promising, he would fly back. For the spot where he had spent the night had some shelter. It also had water, though this was muddy stuff, that made him shudder when he drank it, even after it had been boiled.

He had gone through many periods of excitement since leaving Croydon, but the excitement of that quarter-hour was the most striking of the lot. After fourteen-and-a-half minutes—half a minute to go—he had seen nothing. He was just flying across a little creek. He had almost made up his mind to fly back to the spot where he had spent the night. Then he had the idea that he would cross this little creek, and fly along its far bank.

No sooner had he done this, than he saw the sudden reflexion of sunlight on a metal roof of some sort. Then another roof. Then another. He peered down from the cockpit and counted them. It was now clear that there were quite a number of houses just down below him. Six or seven houses at least, he could see—a hamlet or small village. This was the first sign of human habitation that he had seen for quite a long time. These people, he told himself, might not have the supply of petrol that he needed so badly. They would probably, at all events, be able to tell him where petrol could be had, and how far he was from the nearest town of any size.

So he landed. He was soon greeted by a voice using the strongest Scots accent he had heard for many a long day. That voice was a most welcome sound in Chichester's ear.

The place he had found was Rocklands Homestead. Comooweal was about four miles away. The place where he had spent the night, he was told, was a so-called waterhole, which was visited only about once every six weeks or so. If he had stayed there, he would probably have been there for a long time to come. His "hunch" that he should fly around and explore for a quarter of an hour or so, had paid off now, and he was among good friends, who were only anxious to help him in every way that they possibly could manage.

He thanked his new friends, who provided him with a meal. Then he flew on the remaining four miles to Comooweal.

The exciting part of the trip was over. What remained was sheer routine. He had now something over 1,300 miles to go before he reached Sydney. But he no longer had the urge to get there quickly. He could do this by easy stages, he told himself. The aim of a thousand miles a day had now left him. He worked out three stages in which he would be able to get to Sydney, and these he followed more or less according to plan.

His arrival at Darwin had been quiet and more or less unheralded. But Sydney made up for this. A group of planes met him and flew in with him. Thousands of people were waiting there.

Francis Chichester was taken completely by surprise by the warmth of his welcome. He had not taken on this flight with any idea of seeking publicity, and he had not known, as he had flown across the world, the amount of space that was being given to his flight by all the great newspapers of almost all countries. So when the waiting thousands cheered at the airport, he was astounded.

He wrote a book on his flight, called *Solo to Sydney*. Afterwards, he thought it not a very good book. But it was dictated, and rushed out by the publishers, so that it was in the bookshops while people still remembered the flight that it described. He had, after all, paid all the expenses of that long and arduous journey, and he felt that he was entitled to do anything that he could in order to make a little money in return.

His journey had, however, brought new ambitions into his mind. These, again, were not really efforts to gain publicity for himself, but efforts to do things which had not been done in anything like the same way by anyone else.

He wanted to complete a flight around the world in the Gipsy Moth. That was one of his new ambitions. He wanted to fly across the Tasman Sea, which separated New Zealand from Australia. That was another.

The Tasman Sea flight was the first on which Chichester had set his heart. How could it be done? Up to that time only one great solo flight over a major ocean had been done—Colonel Lindbergh's flight across the Atlantic. The Tasman Sea was not quite as wide as the Atlantic Ocean—it was about two-thirds as wide. But the Gipsy Moth was not as well equipped as Lindbergh's machine had been. In the main, it would not carry as much fuel.

On the other hand, there were islands in the Tasman Sea. It might be possible to refuel there. Or it might be possible to fit floats to the Gipsy Moth, turning it into a sort of seaplane or flying boat, so that refuelling could be arranged at sea. All these things he pondered at some

E   65

length. The flight across the Tasman Sea had never been done solo; the whole idea seized upon his imagination, and he felt that this was something very much worth attempting.

The two main islands in the Tasman Sea were Norfolk Island, just under six hundred miles from New Zealand, and Earl Howe Island, just under five hundred miles from Sydney. The distance between the two islands was about five hundred and fifty miles. The islands therefore divided the Tasman Sea almost into three equal sections. Was this the best way of carrying out the flight?

By the time he conceived this idea Chichester had gone back to New Zealand and had resumed his business there. He had also joined a volunteer air force group which gave its members a certain amount of training. So he asked the chief of this group if it would be possible to have some training on flying seaplanes. This, he thought, might prepare the way for him. Earl Howe Island had a deep and smooth lagoon on which it would be possible to land a seaplane without too much trouble.

It was agreed that he should take his training on seaplanes instead of ordinary aircraft. It would in any case have been a little stupid to give training in flying an aeroplane to a man who had already flown from Croydon to Sydney. But if he could learn to navigate a seaplane, then he would indeed be something like the complete airman.

There were some special problems in this business of navigating the Tasman Sea, too. The islands were very small. If the slightest bit off course, an aeroplane would be likely to miss them altogether. There were no radio aids in those days, no radar, no way of flying blind, on instruments only, so that a pilot could be sure of hitting the target beyond all doubt. Yet to hit that target beyond all doubt was what Francis Chichester would have to do, if he was not to risk drowning in the waters of the Tasman Sea.

It was therefore no wonder that he spent a long time thinking about this new flight before the definite plan of how it was to be done took shape within his mind. The Gipsy Moth was small and light. A side-wind might put her off course enough to miss the small islands which she was trying to hit. This, too, was a factor that had to be taken into consideration.

He decided that he would have to navigate the Gipsy Moth as a sailor navigates a ship. He would have to take measurements of the position of the sun, and steer by that. So, quite cheerfully, he began to teach himself such methods.

Now there was another new problem. The business, which had flourished very much, and had, in a sense, provided the money for the flight from England to Australia, ran into difficulties. There was a slump in the business world, and people were not so anxious to buy land as they had been. To buy the floats and to convert the Gipsy Moth into a seaplane would cost something like £500, and there was not £500 available. All the money that the business possessed was tied up in land and trees and houses.

Yet Francis Chichester never admitted defeat. When he was faced with any difficulty, whether it was a difficulty of engineering or a difficulty of money, he always knew that there was a possibility of getting out of it. He had set his heart on flying across the Tasman Sea, and fly across the Tasman Sea he would. At this time, too, there was a successful flight across the sea by an Australian, called Menzies. But he flew from Australia to

New Zealand. No one had flown it in the opposite direction. Chichester had now made up his mind to be the first man in the world to do this.

That London to Australia flight had given him the urge to do all sorts of things. More than ever, now, was he the lone adventurer, bent on doing things by himself alone which had never before been achieved. He worried various government officials, to see if it would be possible to borrow a pair of floats which had been discarded by some other machine. For a time he did not succeed; but finally he persuaded the government to make the loan.

So now, at any rate in theory, he was all set for this attempt on a new flight. He knew that there would be an awful lot of practical work to be done, before he could set off. The actual conversion of the machine, for example, would not be at all easy, but he was fully confident that it could be done.

One experienced seaplane pilot whom Chichester had got to know, warned him that it would not be as easy going as he might think. The Gipsy Moth would have to be very heavily loaded—in the main with fuel—and it would not be easy to take off from the surface of the sea, particularly if it was at all rough, or if there was a heavy swell on. Wind directions might be difficult in this connexion.

Francis Chichester did not allow himself to be put off by this warning, however. He had made up his mind to have a shot at this flight across the Tasman Sea, and it should by this time be quite clear that when Francis Chichester had made up his mind to do something, he usually went through with it, despite all the difficulties.

He had flown the Gipsy Moth something like 34,000 miles as an ordinary aeroplane, and to turn a landplane into a seaplane after this amount of flying was something that had almost certainly never been tried by anyone else.

However, the conversion was not such a difficult job as had been feared. It did not seem long before the machine was wheeled down the slipway into the harbour on a huge trolley. She floated well. Chichester got on board, started off the engines, and found that the machine took off from the surface of the water without any difficulty at all. He was very delighted at this result. His friend, however, warned him that he should not take it for granted from this that things would always be so easy. He had, as it happened, struck a day when conditions were just right. There was a fairly strong wind, and he could take off against this; the tide was with him. They had not tested the floats fully, to make sure that they did not leak. There were many precautions to take. But Chichester did not let any of these things disturb him at all. He was quite sure now that all would go well.

So he ignored the need to test the floats. He also grinned when he was told that he ought to have some test flights, to make sure that his navigational knowledge was good enough for this long flight across sea. If he had taken any notice of such remarks, the flight might not have taken place.

He took his rubber dinghy again, and a lot of food and a lot of petrol. A friend who was a radio engineer had built for him a tiny transmitting set. This friend had been quite horrified to learn that the long flight from Europe to Australia had been undertaken without any means of communicating with the outside world. This was a set so small that it weighed only 23 pounds; but it was powerful enough to enable Chichester to send out messages if he got into any real difficulties.

This was not as valuable as had been thought; there were few ships normally on the Tasman Sea. He promised, however, to try to send out a signal every hour, and then his New Zealand friends would know that he was all right.

He intended to start at six o'clock in the morning. His friends, who were more or less expert mechanics, insisted on all sorts of tests that they thought were needful. But when the hour of 6.15 was reached, Chichester lost patience. So off he took, making a smooth and successful start. As he climbed into the sky, he tapped on his radio set, time after time, the Morse signal: "Can you hear me?" For a time there was no reply, and he thought that, after all, the set wasn't working. But finally a light glowed on the set. This meant that a reply was coming.

All was well, then, he told himself. Another great adventure was starting. It was good to be up there, on his own, and to know that what happened now would be completely a matter for himself. The lone adventurer had everything in his own hands again, and this was just how he liked it.

He had roughly twelve hours of daylight, and he considered that for ten of these twelve hours he would be in the air. For the first three of those hours he would be flying along the New Zealand coast, and had planned to refuel at the northernmost tip of the Dominion.

He used the sun, as he had planned, to give him direction. He had to take readings on a sextant, in order to do this. Yet at the same time he had to hang on to the controls. When the Gipsy Moth had been a landplane she had been fairly stable in the air. But the heavy floats now meant that if he let go of the levers she tended to dip

down towards the sea. Flying was much more difficult
than it had previously been. He had to get used to all
this while he was flying along the coast of New Zealand,
so that, if there was any real difficulty, he would be able
to come down on the surface of the sea with comparative
safety, and not a hundred miles from the nearest land.

His navigation, he feared, was not as good as had
been hoped. But he found the northern tip of New
Zealand, and the spot where he had been intending to
pick up his supply of petrol. Here he found the harbour
to have water far too shallow to risk landing in. He
surfaced a little out from the harbour, and threw down
an anchor. But the seaplane drifted. The anchor was not
heavy enough, or secure enough, to hold the Gipsy Moth
in position. A man and a boy took off from the harbour
in a small boat, and he shouted, asking if they had an
anchor. Then he asked about his petrol, and they said
that they had not expected him so soon.

Chichester was getting anxious. The precious minutes
of daylight were ticking away, and he did not want to
risk losing time, since it would mean that he would be
flying over an unfamiliar stretch of sea, looking for an
island he had never before seen from the air. And this
would be in darkness, if he did not soon get his store of
petrol and get away. It was a very anxious period, and
yet he knew that it was of no use at all getting impatient
about it. This man from the shore would not, after all,
know how closely he was working to a time-table.

When a good deal of time had elapsed, the petrol was
brought out. Chichester kept looking at his watch.

The man asked where he was going. Chichester told
him that he was bound for Australia. When told that
this was 1,500 miles away, the man commented that it

was a long swim. Chichester said that he was planning to get to Norfolk Island that night, and that this was about 500 miles; the man said that this was a long swim too.

Time was going on. But Chichester now had another twelve gallons of precious petrol in his tanks. In a matter of minutes he was off, though not without some difficulty. At first Gipsy Moth seemed very reluctant to rise. Still, by midday he left the New Zealand coast, and headed out to sea.

Now he was dependent on his self-taught methods of navigation. He had also to allow for the fact that the wind might tend to drive him to some extent off his course. Norfolk Island was small, and it would be very easy to miss it if he made any mistakes.

He ran into dark clouds. Beneath him was the sea. No land at all was in sight. He had moments of fear, when he wondered what would happen if, after all, his sextant readings had been in error. With the sun hidden behind the clouds, he could not make any measurements for some time. Then it came through a gap in the clouds, and he made a hasty reading. It seemed that his calculations had been correct. This reading was just what he had expected, and he flew on with a good deal more confidence in his mind.

He was now headed straight for the island, and before long it came in sight. All was well. He had made his first hop successfully. He wondered where would be the best place to come down. There was a fairly heavy swell on the sea, as he could detect on dropping closer to it. He had to select a bay where there was some shelter from the wind. If he landed on a choppy sea the machine might be badly damaged.

The first little bay that he selected was no good. The air was bumpy, and as he coasted in over the cliff-top, the aeroplane plunged down suddenly, and Chichester was shot out of his seat. He managed to climb again and made for the next bay. Here he landed smoothly and easily. The first lap was over.

He stayed that night in the house of the Governor. He did not sleep well, for he was thinking of the Gipsy Moth, and wondering what would happen if a high wind sprang up in the night. The bay was hardly protected at all from the open sea, and if it got really stormy the aeroplane might be crushed against the shore. Fuelling, too, was not easy, as the Gipsy Moth swung about. Chichester had to take four-gallon tins of petrol and pour the fluid into the tanks. A lot of it got spilled in the process.

Taking off in the morning was a nightmare. First of all, one of the cylinders of the engine refused to fire. Then, when Chichester got the engine going, the Gipsy Moth just would not rise from the water. There was a considerable swell on the surface, and he found that this was enough to make it impossible to get the lift that was necessary. He ran on the surface of the water to another little bay, but this seemed no better. Then he found that the floats had leaked, and there was water in them. There was no way of baling this out. The only way was to put a tube down from the inside of the machine and suck the water out, then spitting it overboard.

Chichester did this for what seemed to be hours. He calculated that he must have sucked out gallons of water. When finally he did get clear of the water he saw a flash of metal wire in the air, and the Gipsy Moth plunged back to the sea again.

He knew what had happened. There were wire struts

which connected the floats together. One of these had snapped. There was only one thing to do. He would have to go back to the harbour where he had spent the night, and see if the broken wire could be somehow repaired. But was this possible? For the first time he felt real doubts about the whole enterprise.

In the end he made it and the wire was repaired. But still there was the problem of getting airborne again. On Norfolk Island there was a man named Brent, who was a first-rate mechanic, and he helped Chichester with the question of how the water had got into the floats. This was clearly what caused the trouble in take-off. Brent did his best over this. They filled the floats with water, and none leaked out. The only place that the water could have got in was at the top, where metal plates were fitted. Brent fixed the plates more firmly, and thought that this would settle that difficulty. Long afterwards they found that it had not settled the difficulty, which had really been due to a stainless steel plate pulling away from the thin aluminium sides of the floats.

However, after some more adjustments, Chichester succeeded in getting into the air and set off for Earl Howe Island. Here there were more troubles. The worst of these was that the screws holding the compass into position worked lose, which meant that the compass swung around.

He still made measurements of the position of the sun and tried to fly by means of his sextant readings. But the distance was about six hundred miles, and again there was the problem that a slight error in navigation would put him well off his target.

When he was about halfway between the islands the machine started to vibrate furiously. It was these vibrations that caused the compass to come unstuck. The only explanation that Chichester could think of was that the propeller was waggling on its shaft. The aeroplane went on moving fairly steadily forward; but he could not help wondering what would happen to the shaky propeller if he struck any violent sidewinds.

He did not meet these for a time, at any rate. He ran into heavy clouds and heavy rain instead. This meant that he could not take his readings of the sun position for some time. With the compass out of action, this made accurate navigation almost impossible. He had a little pocket compass; but to hold this steady, with the violent shaking, was more difficult than he had imagined it could be. He was now very worried indeed. He had gone so far that he should be at any rate in sight of Earl Howe Island. He gazed at the horizon, but no island was to be seen. Had me made some silly mistake? Was he badly off course? He could not be sure of this, and his worries grew greater.

Then there came a break in the cloud. The sun shone through. Rapidly adjusting his instruments, he measured direction. It seemed that he was heading straight for the island!

Soon he was in another rain-cloud. As he flew out of it his worries vanished altogether. There was land straight ahead. He had found Earl Howe Island, and all his worries had been without foundation.

Getting down was not at all easy. But get down somehow he did, though there was a squally wind. He crawled ashore and went to bed.

It was the next morning that tragedy struck. As he walked down to the harbour towards the spot where he had moored the machine, it was nowhere to be seen.

He looked around in amazement. What had happened?
And then he saw. Only the tail of the machine was
showing. It had been hit by a storm in the night, and
had sunk beneath the water.

CHAPTER SIX

STARTING AGAIN

A LESSER man would have been knocked sideways by this. Not so Francis Chichester. He went back, had some breakfast, and then sat down to consider what to do. Here he was, on a small island in the middle of the Tasman Sea. His machine was under water, and no one could say how much it might have been damaged. Australia was hundreds of miles away. There was also to be remembered that the propeller had been behaving curiously before the tragedy of the night. It was certain that being immersed in salt water would not have helped that matter.

They got the machine out of the water in the end, and Chichester thought he knew the worst. The wings were crumpled, the engine looked a wreck, the fuselage did not appear as if it would ever again be airworthy. To begin with, he felt that only the floats were any good, and that the rest of the machine would have to be sold as scrap. Even that would not be easy, as there were no scrap-metal merchants on the island.

Chichester had set out alone from Auckland. He wanted to arrive alone in Australia. He felt that it would be letting himself down if he simply travelled on the little steamer that sailed over the Tasman Sea. He would rather get a small boat and finish the job solo in that way. But then he had a brainwave. There did not seem to be any pieces of the machine hopelessly badly damaged. Why not try to rebuild the aeroplane on Earl Howe Island, so that he could set off again in due course, and finish the job that he had begun so eagerly when he left New Zealand?

It seemed a crazy idea at first. But he looked at the parts into which the machine had been broken down, and it began to seem more and more possible. Some spare parts would be needed, of course, but not as many as had at first seemed likely. Could the seaplane be rebuilt there and then? A good deal of the bodywork was wood, and could be replaced if necessary. The great point was the engine. As he studied it, he thought that it could be made to work again. Why not? A great wave of excitement came over him. Perhaps it would be possible. Perhaps, after all, he would complete his flight across the Tasman Sea.

Dignam, the man who was to have given Chichester the petrol for the later part of his journey, was soon as eager as Chichester himself to get the machine in the air again. He promised to help in every way possible, and see if the battered Gipsy Moth could be made airworthy.

When the steamer arrived, they had worked out a list of the spare parts that they would need. This list was sent to Sydney, with a request that these spares should be sent back on the return journey. Meanwhile they got on with such beginnings of the rebuilding as they could. Chichester knew that time was short. They could not take too long over the task, or they would run into the storms of winter, which were very bad around the island. Then he would be stuck on that isolated little island for months.

However, the spares arrived as requested, and the job

of rebuilding went on apace. They had to paint the wings with what was called "dope". This is a kind of waterproof paint, and several coats of it had to be put on. There were certain specified temperatures at which the "dope" had to be put on, and for a time they found this not easy, with the result that the paint did not go on evenly. In the end they mastered this, and many other jobs which were needful.

The actual rebuilding had been done on a bank, above the sandy beach. When the task was complete, there was a new difficulty about which they had not thought. The Gipsy Moth was ready for launching. But how was she to be launched?

There was a drop of about six feet between the bank and the beach. If she were pushed over the edge, something would get smashed again. The machine weighed about half a ton, and one of Chichester's friends, who had helped on the work, suggested that they should carry her down to the edge of the water.

"Carry her?" Chichester said in astonishment.

"Why not?"

Chichester was puzzled. "How can we carry something weighing half a ton?" he asked.

In the end the seaplane *was* carried. It was done by putting some hefty beams under the four floats, and having four men to hold each of the beams. There were thus sixteen men to lift the machine. Then one man stood by, like the conductor of an orchestra, Chichester said. He gave them the signal to lift or to put down, and the sixteen men worked as a team under his direction.

The scheme worked. In the end the seaplane was on the water and afloat. When Chichester thought of the way in which she had been damaged on his arrival at

79

Earl Howe Island, he felt that this was something very like a miracle.

The first trial flight was not a success. The Gipsy Moth flew only for a few yards, and then the engine stopped. But this was only due to a choked tube. When all the tubes were carefully cleaned, she flew as well as ever she had done, and Chichester heaved a sigh of great relief.

He had made up his mind to fly direct to Sydney, which was not much short of 500 miles. He could have shortened the journey, and landed at a nearer spot on the Australian mainland; but Sydney it had to be. His last night on Earl Howe Island was a peaceful one. The weather was calm, and he had made up his mind that this was a time of "now or never". He slept like a top, and woke in the morning fresh and calm.

The take-off was not good. It seemed that the machine did not respond to the controls as well as it had formerly done, and to begin with Chichester wondered if after all there had been some faults in their rebuilding. He had filled with fuel to the limits that the tanks would take, and he now had the idea of letting some of this petrol run away, so that he would lighten the load that had to be got into the air. He had to jettison quite a lot before the machine rose. When he was fully airborne, he looked at the petrol gauge. He had enough fuel left for about eight hours' flying. This would be all right if the conditions were good. But if he ran into strong head-winds, his speed would be slowed down. Then it might be that the petrol would not last out.

Having got so far, he was not going to turn back. This was a risk that he had to take. Chichester sometimes gambled with fate, and this was in some respects the greatest gamble of his life so far. After all, he told himself, it was no longer, as it had been with the islands, a matter of hitting a tiny target in a vast expanse of sea. Australia was nearly 2,000 miles long. He would have to be a mighty bad navigator who could not hit a target of that size!

So he settled down to the old routine of watching progress, checking position, reading off distances, observing speed. It seemed a long time since he had last done this. Now he had the pleasant feeling that he was on the final stage of a perilous journey, and that the worst of the journey was almost certainly behind him. There were still moments when the engine gave him some cause for anxiety. Yet when it appeared not to be running smoothly, it sooner or later got back to its normal even sound, and he was able to breathe freely again.

Once again he ran into rain. It was one of the heaviest rainstorms that he had ever flown through. There was a strong north wind, too, and he felt that he was flying almost sideways over the sea. He could see the rainwater pouring off the edges of the wings, and in the open cockpit where he was sitting he got soaked to the skin.

The storm got steadily worse. At one point Chichester saw a ship below him. He flew a bit lower, to see if he could get into wireless communication with the crew. There was not a sign of life on the ship. She was wallowing in giant waves. She must have been abandoned by her crew, but no lifeboats were anywhere to be seen.

The Gipsy Moth was making heavy going. Now and then the engine would splutter. Water must have been getting into it from time to time. But still the aircraft kept going, though it was now almost impossible for Chichester to be sure of his position or the direction in which he was flying. He tried to get out a chart which he was carrying. But the chart was soaking wet and he could not unfold it properly. He felt grimly determined to hang on somehow.

When he had left Earl Howe Island he had calculated that he had eight hours' supply of petrol, and it was after six hours' flying time that the rain abated a little. Peering ahead of him, he thought that he could see land. He wondered if he was imagining things. He had imagined himself as seeing all sorts of strange objects at points along his journey, and now he felt that this might just be another illusion. He scarcely dared to look in the forward direction again, and he steeled himself not to do so for ten minutes. When the ten minutes had passed he looked ahead.

Yes. It was land. This was Australia. He had managed that flight across the Tasman Sea, in spite of the damage to his aircraft, in spite of the frightful weather through which he had now been flying for hours. In a patched-up wreck of a seaplane he had made the crossing. He felt elated and yet in a way at the same time he felt that the greatest moment of his life had passed. When he had been battling with the storm, he had hardly had time to think. Now he could almost sit back and think, he had a sense that the lonely adventure was over and that before long he would be settling down to a dull routine once again. In the bay that now lay below him he could see some ships at anchor. They were units of the Australian Navy. He longed to fly down, talk to the sailors, have the joy of human company again, after the battle of the last few hours. He had been fighting the wind and the rain for so long that some warm sympathy was what he needed more than anything else.

But he had told himself, when setting out, that he was

going to fly direct to Sydney, not to some remote spot on the Australian coast, miles from anywhere. He glanced at his petrol gauge. He had enough fuel for some distance longer. It would, he told himself, be quite possible to get to Sydney on his remaining petrol. Why not stick to his original plan, and finish the flight in Sydney harbour?

However, he might as well drop down here and find out precisely how far he had to go. He came down to the surface of the sea and switched off his engine. The silence was uncanny, after all those hours of storm—not to mention the continuous roar of the engines of the Gipsy Moth. All that he could hear was the slap of the ripples against the floats of his seaplane, and against the vast bulk of the warship not far away.

He stood up and waved. Soon a lamp flashed from the deck of the ship. Then a small motor-boat left the ship and drew close. Chichester asked the crew of the boat the distance to Sydney. They told him it was about eighty miles. Again he looked at his fuel. He had enough to do well over eighty miles.

But the Gipsy Moth would not take off. Chichester swallowed his pride, and asked the men in the motor boat if they would give him a tow. They pulled him without much difficulty, and soon he was climbing up the ladder on the Australian ship *Albatross*.

The *Albatross* was an aircraft carrier. One of the officers on board volunteered to make all the necessary arrangements to lift the Gipsy Moth on board. Chichester was not very excited now. Indeed, he felt a bit depressed. He himself has said that after his greatest adventures he has felt depression. The joy for him has been in the difficulties faced and overcome. When they are actually overcome the joy has often suddenly departed.

So it was now. What made it worse was that, in hooking the aircraft on to the great cable that was to haul it on board the *Albatross* Chichester crushed his right hand. He needed medical attention, but he landed in Sydney fit and well, though minus the tip of one finger.

This would have been thought to be enough adventure for one man. He had flown from England to New Zealand. He had flown across the Tasman Sea. He had defied fate and won through against the most terrifying odds. But when once such ambitions have got a grip on a man, they do not easily let him go.

Some months earlier, in Auckland, Chichester had formulated two ambitions which he wanted to see fulfilled before long. One was to fly across the Tasman Sea. This he had now done. The other was to fly around the world. He had, in effect, done half this journey, in his flight from England to Australia. Should he attempt the other half of the journey, and fly back by the opposite route?

In Sydney he thought about this at great length. The journey would be to a large extent overland, if he ever attempted it. Since his machine had been converted into a seaplane, this meant that he would have to work out a route which would allow him, every 500 miles or so, to come down on sea, lake, or river. That was not at all an easy thing to get worked out, as he well knew. Moreover, he would have to know in advance just where he was going to come down, in order to get permission to come down at his selected spots. From his flight from England to Australia, he had come to know that this was not always as easy as it might seem on the surface. Sometimes people were awkward about such matters. Sometimes they were afraid that the world traveller was a spy. So, before he could consider any such flight around the other half of the world, there was an awful lot of planning to be done.

As soon as the Australian Navy had landed him in Sydney, on the completion of the Tasman Sea flight, Chichester was therefore making inquiries and thinking about this new enterprise.

He knew that he would have to fly northwards over the Pacific, landing in Japan. He might have to fly across China. It was an exciting new adventure, and it was not long before he was deep in his preparations. He planned to reach England; but he would not do this from the South, as would happen if he retraced his footsteps of the outward journey. He would approach it from the East. This meant going over some countries with which Great Britain was not on particularly friendly terms. It also meant that there might be places where refuelling bases would be very difficult to find.

The first stage, he decided, would certainly be to get to Japan. There were, of course, a number of islands which would provide intermediate steps. But many of these at that time were owned by Holland. The Dutch Government were friendly enough. They welcomed visitors. But they did not welcome visitors who might owing to some mishap become a charge on the Dutch Colonial Office. New Guinea was particularly awkward territory, and they said that if Chichester wanted to fly that way, he would have to guarantee that if there was any expense in looking after him, he would repay it in some way. Chichester's comment was that if he crash-landed in New Guinea, he might find himself condemned to work for the Dutch Government for the rest of his life, in order to repay the expenses.

Gradually, however, his plans took shape. There was

a long correspondence to be carried on with various governments. He now knew that his previous flights, though they had in the end turned out well enough, yet involved some pretty haphazard work, and that much more detailed planning would be advisable for the future.

Australia to Japan was a long journey—though he had done longer ones. In order to pull this off, he would have to divide up the distance into conveniently short hops, and have arrangements for refuelling worked out at each spot at which he was going to stop.

Naturally, he could not plan for too many emergencies. It was no good taking for granted that there would be such calamities as his aeroplane damage at Earl Howe Island. If one expected such difficulties as that, then one would not attempt the flight at all. Yet he had to be ready for whatever might happen, and he knew that the secret of success in this world of long-distance flying was boldness.

It was late June in 1931 before his preparations were complete. Then he thought that he could work out the journey without too many qualms. It was, of course, winter in Australia. But long before he got to Japan it would be warm and summery. He planned to leave Sydney on July 3, to fly more or less around the Australian coast, and then hop along the islands across the Pacific, eventually arriving in Japan sometime in August. There had never been a solo flight between Australia and Japan. Nor had there been a seaplane flight, solo or otherwise, between the two countries.

He now felt greater confidence than ever before in the performance that the Gipsy Moth was likely to be able to put up. The engine had been overhauled and reconditioned. Many cracks and other faults had been found.

When he had read the engineers' report on the state of the engine, Chichester was astonished to think that he had ever been able to fly the length of the Tasman Sea. Now all these things had been righted, and he should be able to face the next stage in his adventurous journeyings quite happily.

He slept quite well on his last night on Australian soil. The machine had been made ready with the utmost care.

Usually, when setting out on some new journey, there had been anxieties in Chichester's mind. There were none now. He climbed into the cockpit of the Gipsy Moth, got the engine started. It made a satisfying roar, and he knew that this time he had an engine in first-rate condition to hurry him on his way. As he flew above Sydney Harbour, and looked down at the impressive bridge below, he felt that urge of delight that always came into his heart at a new lone adventure.

CHAPTER SEVEN

JAPANESE JOURNEY

THE first part of this new flight, along the Australian coast, above the Great Barrier Reef, was almost dull. He could see the coastline, stretching away below him, mile after mile of it. He came down once or twice at his agreed refuelling points. His plans had been well laid. The only relief from the sheer mechanics of flying was the natural life which he could watch. Sometimes, for instance, he saw flamingoes flying past.

At a little town called Rockhampton, which was one of his refuelling points, he found some difficulty in taking off from the river. He had an enjoyable evening first, walking through the streets, with their puffing little steam trams, and then being entertained to beer, and asked to answer all sorts of questions from some of the local people.

More than once he felt sleepy while flying. This was always one of the hazards of flying long distances alone. He slept well when he landed, but when, next day, he had flown some hundreds of miles, he found sleep making him heavy-eyed. He knew, however, that it was of no use making any landing at a spot not planned for. This would upset his timing, and it might well be that if he came down in the wrong place, he might find take-off impossible.

In spite of the Dutch warnings, he had arranged for

one stop in New Guinea, at a place called Merauke. He found this to be more or less an area cleared from dense jungle, and he began to understand why the Dutch Government had been so reluctant to allow him to fly over this island. He bought some petrol from a store kept by a Chinese. It was in tins that had no maker's name on them.

For a thousand miles ahead Chichester had no map or chart. He had hoped to be able to buy a map, and as he wandered around the streets and looked at the flimsy-looking shops built of bamboo, he wondered what chance there was of buying one. There was none to be found, and he was worried. In the end he talked to a Dutch official, and this man kindly gave Chichester a map of his own.

He slept a night there. But it was hot and sticky. In the morning he found taking-off difficult, with the river surface smooth and the air moist. In the end the Gipsy Moth was airborne, but he was whole-heartedly glad to leave New Guinea behind him.

Five hours and nearly five hundred miles later he came down at a small island called Dobo. Here a launch with four men on board came close to the seaplane. On New Guinea scarcely anyone had been able to speak English. He was now delighted to hear these men doing just that. But they did not come very near, though Chichester shouted to them.

Presently a Dutch Government boat came alongside, and he was taken in this boat to the jetty to fetch his petrol. Thousands of natives stood on the quay, and as Chichester came in sight they cheered loudly and madly.

Now there came more island-hopping. Again it was not very exciting. Chichester had gone through so many perils on his previous journeys that he began to wonder if it was not possible to plan things too thoroughly, and if this did not mean that even his kind of adventurous journeys might not in the end become something of a bore, however exciting they might appear to be to the outside world. Time after time, when he came to some island, where he had decided that petrol would be available—and also fresh water—he found that it worked so smoothly that he might almost have been in Australia or England. It was only the houses and the people and the enveloping jungle scenery that made it clear to him that he was in a remote island on the very edge of civilisation, and not in a highly populated and busy centre of trade.

At Amboina—another of the Pacific Islands—he had found that the river mouth on which he had come down did not give him enough space to take off again. He got some of the inhabitants to tow him out to sea. It was choppy, and it was not easy to take off, and he threw overboard all that he could, in order to save weight. Then he discovered, to his horror, that he had, in jettisoning all this extra weight, even thrown away the map on which he was depending for his flight for the next hundred miles or more. His own maps, which he had prepared before leaving Sydney, did not cover in detail some of the island-hopping journeys.

He even found one island, with a high range of mountains, which had not been on his map at all, and he wondered if he had made some mistake in his navigation, and had flown far off course. He managed to get over the mountains and flew on. Now he ran into a tropical rainstorm, which almost destroyed visibility, and he had to fly blind until he left the storm behind him.

After a period during which the engine cut out once or twice, bringing his heart into his mouth, he reached the Philippines. A man brought out a bag of letters, saying that they wanted him to take them on. When Chichester explained that he had come down to take petrol, the man said: "There is no petrol here."

Francis Chichester was staggered. He did not think, in this modern world, there could possibly be a place of any size where no petrol at all was available. He asked to be taken to some government official. This man repeated that there was no petrol, and then asked if Chichester could not use gasoline instead. The word "petrol" was not known to them. They always used the American term "gasoline" for it.

Here he was granted an interview with the president, who gave him what Chichester described as the finest cigar he had ever smoked. It was, in a way, a waste of time, but, as he was dependent on the Filipinos for petrol, he thought he ought to be as polite as possible to the authorities.

At least, he was progressing, and there had been no serious mishaps as yet. Australia now seemed a long way behind him. But Japan seemed an equally long way ahead.

Chichester slept soundly enough at the beginning of the night. Then the house began to quiver and shake. He sat up in bed with a start. It was an earthquake, and through the night he counted no fewer than eleven separate tremors.

The next morning he hunted for petrol. At first he had no success, but in the end he had twelve gallons given to him by the town authorities. So his memories from the Philippines were very mixed.

He was not to leave the Philippines for awhile. His propellor was damaged and had to be repaired. Also one of the floats was again flooded with water. This was the fault that had given trouble for a long time, and it was not yet dealt with. He was thinking of flying back to England. He was only one-third of the way around the world, and he had already been on this lonely flight for months. No wonder that he felt despondent sometimes.

Eventually, with propeller and floats repaired, he took off and headed north, towards Japan. This meant that he was nearing the end of the first stage. The Japanese Government had forbidden him to land in certain areas, so he had to be very careful over this. At one spot where water for his landing had been very carefully stated, he found high cliffs, which would have made landing dangerous. After the long and tiresome journey from the Philippines to the Japanese coast, this was very annoying.

When in the end he did get down on Japanese territory he was surprised to find flags flying and Japanese crowds cheering. He had never thought to find such a ceremonial welcome.

He had one worth-while experience there, however. A mechanic, called in to inspect the float which had so many times filled with water, traced the trouble. Screws used to fix it to the hull had been left a little loose. When the float was racing through water, as it was prior to take-off, water rushed in, to slop about inside the float as soon as the machine got into the air. So that was one of Chichester's real headaches finally dealt with.

Japan he really saw only for a short time. He was anxious to be farther on his way. He had heard rumours of typhoons, but did not really believe them, as the official weather forecasts sounded cheerful enough. China was his next country, in the days before the modern Chinese Communists had control. Looking down over the Chinese coast, he wondered where he would be able to come down. Every worth-while harbour seemed to be full of boats of one sort or another. When in the end he did find a small patch of smooth water, and came into it, hundreds of junks seemed to be sailing towards the Gipsy Moth.

He soon took off again and made for Shanghai, which he found a much more go-ahead and modern place than the spots he had first found in China. A South African journalist, working for the *North China News*, asked him for an interview. Chichester now realised that his fame had spread even to quite remote spots. Even though Shanghai was a big place, it was a long way from both England and Australia. Yet his name was known in all these places.

His experience of Japan up to now had been limited to the outlying islands—notably Formosa, which was then Japanese, though later China was to possess it. But, after flying over part of China, he had to continue towards the main island of Japan. He still heard rumours of a typhoon; but still he did not take much notice. He had flown through so much bad weather that he was not very worried about future weather, no matter how bad it might be.

If the typhoon was such that he could not reach the Japanese mainland, he could always go towards Korea. Chichester studied maps. He would be going in the right general direction, no matter which country he made his next port of call, he thought. He was used to making up his mind about things as he went along. One or two people to whom he spoke in Shanghai were very worried about this, but he was not.

After he had taken off, he found that winds were strong, but not frighteningly so. He ate some chicken, which he had taken up with him. Now his speed indicator broke down and so he was not able to calculate how far he had flown since leaving Shanghai. He had, as always, kept his fuel down to the minimum, in order to fly light, and he wondered if he had enough to get him to the Japanese coast.

By now the sea was calm. The sky looked an odd colour. Chichester, for the first time that day, felt worried. Was there really a typhoon about? Was the period he was now going through the calm before the storm?

He had been told of a Japanese fishing port called Katsuura, where he would be able to touch down in a natural harbour, and where petrol would probably be available. He thought that he had enough fuel to get him there. He was mightily relieved when he found the place. He had a sense of triumph. He had not been scared off by the rumoured typhoon, and had fought his way across to the Japanese mainland, touching China on the way. He was a happy man when he went to bed in that little Japanese town that night.

The next morning came disaster. His host of the night had asked him to fly around the town before making off, as the townspeople would like to have a good view of the Gipsy Moth. This Chichester had agreed to do. But no one had thought of warning him that, stretched from the harbour to a high spot in the town were some telephone wires. In making his circuit of the town, he flew straight into these.

All that he knew at the time was a sense of a tremendous

crash, the seaplane sinking like a stone, and then unconsciousness.

He was carried to hospital. The best medical treatment was given him. For a time it was thought that he might be blind, but the skill of the Japanese doctors saved his eyes.

This was, however, for the time the end of his flight. The Gipsy Moth was hopelessly smashed, and he gave the pieces to a local school, for use by boys who might be interested in engineering. Then he began to wonder if he could get back to England, by air, by sea, by any method at all.

In the end he went to Kobe by a little local steamer, and from there took passage on a large liner to England. It was not the way that he had planned to come home, but he knew that he would not be able to rebuild the Gipsy Moth a second time. She was too thoroughly smashed for that.

It was good to be back in his home territory of North Devon after all the adventures he had gone through. He settled down with friends in the little Devonshire town of Instow, and wrote a book about his flight across the Tasman Sea. He was given a trophy awarded to airmen for special feats of endurance and courage—this for his Tasman Sea flight. It seemed that it was that flight which people would remember him for. If anyone at that time had told Francis Chichester that he would in the end get even greater fame for a masterly sea voyage he would have laughed at the idea. To him, then, there was only one way of travelling across the world, and that was by air. Ships were slow and old-fashioned and unsatisfactory.

Still, it was by ship that he went back to New Zealand,

to start again with the business which he had helped to build up before his adventurous flights. Again it brought a queer sensation into his mind to be looking after the routines of business when he thought of Earl Howe Island and Katsuura. They both seemed so far away from the office in Wellington that they appeared like another world.

He jumped at the opportunity of another flight. This time it was not to be a solo one. He had a friend called Frank Herrick, who had the idea of flying to England. Chichester eagerly worked out a scheme. They bought a Puss Moth machine, and decided that they would try it.

There had been a long and quiet interlude before this. For nearly four years Chichester had worked in the office, finding his greatest relaxation in fishing. He had not flown for all that time, and now he was almost like a child with a new toy.

This was a simpler flight, in some respects, than any he had done before. It led him through some pretty familiar spots. By now there were main airline routes across the globe. They did not intend to use these, but thought that they would fly across Siberia. But the Russian authorities would not permit it. They skirted what was then Indo-China, calling at a place called Hanoi, which was to be much in the news many years later. Then they got on a normal commercial route, through India into Egypt, and Chichester recorded without much pleasure that it took him only twenty-nine and a half hours from Cairo to Brooklands.

This was not what he really thought of as flying. Perhaps he felt that, with a passenger in his hands, he could not take the sort of chances that he did when he was on his own. Or perhaps it was merely that Francis

Chichester, all through his life, was not the sort of person who would get into a rut. If he did get into a rut, he found that life was dull.

He did not find life dull in England, however. For it was here that he met Sheila Craven, whom he married. He took her out to New Zealand in 1937, but the visit was not a success. Chichester still had an interest in the business there, but she did not like the country very much to begin with, and soon they were on their way back to Europe—this time in a perfectly ordinary liner and not in an aeroplane.

One reason why they came back was that Chichester was sure that war with Germany was on the way, and he thought that his experience with aeroplanes would be of value to the British Government. He tried to join the Royal Air Force as a fighter pilot. All this was a long way from his experiences of a few short years before. But he felt that if he could navigate an aeroplane as he had done in the early 1930s, he would be a useful person in the air battles that would no doubt come if war broke out.

He was told that at the age of thirty-seven he was too old for flying duties in the R.A.F. This seemed to him absurd, but he could not argue with the authorities. He got a post with a firm, where his main task was checking bubble sextants. It was a queer sensation to be working for someone else—something he had not done for about sixteen years. The adventurous spirit which was Francis Chichester's felt stifled in this post. Yet what else could he do?

When the air raids on London started, he wrote a book explaining how to spot enemy aircraft. It sold in large numbers. He followed this up with other books of a similar kind, and then he was asked to join the R.A.F.

as an officer, in order to write booklets on navigation for young and untrained pilots. He was appointed a Flying Officer as soon as this task was agreed.

All this was another strange contrast with his adventurous peacetime life. Chichester must be one of the few active souls who found adventure in peace and dullness in war. He considered that he wrote something like half a million words on aircraft navigation in those war years, when he would much rather have been doing some active duty. But it was not to be.

His sight was never good. This barred him from flying duties. Wherever he went in the R.A.F. he never got anything by what he thought of as a job at a desk, and not at the controls of an aeroplane. Soon this was to some extent altered, as he was given the task of helping young men with the problems of air navigation, and one of his chiefs said that it was silly expecting a man to do this if he had not flown for years himself.

So Chichester started flying again, with many different types of machine. He even had a little solo machine for his own use, with which he could work out practice routes to be used by the young men who were in part his students. He got much joy out of this, even though in the later part of the war, when the so-called "flying bombs" were developed by the Germans, he had anxious moments, both for his little machine, and for his wife, left in their London home while he was at some country airfield.

He had invented a game called "Pinpoint the Bomber" which had been moderately successful during the war. When the war ended, and he had left the forces, he had a lot of maps which had been part of this game. He got them stuck on board, cut them into pieces, and sold them, highly successfully, as map jigsaw puzzles. He had never been content to work as an employee for someone else. He had spent most of his money on his travels before the war, and his war work had not been highly paid.

His jigsaw puzzles paid well. He sold some thousands of them. Then sales dropped off, and he decided to produce a new map. This again sold for a time. He had the idea of producing a new map jigsaw every few months. Then one day a man came in and said that a picture map of London which had been the basis of one of Chichester's jigsaw puzzles was one of the most attractive maps he had seen. If it were not stuck on a piece of board, he would be prepared to buy five thousand copies. Chichester thereupon became a map publisher.

But not a map publisher only. For the time he was making a living by publishing maps. But fate was not content to leave him with that.

CHAPTER EIGHT

THE SAILING LIFE

IT MIGHT have seemed, now, that Francis Chichester's adventures were over. He had made a great name as a flying man. But that appeared to be finished, and he was in the process of building up a business as a publisher of maps. For some years he did much of the office work, typing letters, sending out invoices and all the rest. It was a struggle, as it is bound to be with anyone who starts on a new line of business.

Yet he yearned for a more practical life. The business was building up quite well, but an aeroplane is a costly thing to run. Chichester wanted to do some kind of navigation, but air navigation was beyond what he could afford. Why not, he asked himself, start doing some navigation on the sea? He might be able to afford a boat of some sort—even a small yacht—and then his wife and small son would be able to come with him, and they could have cheerful weekends. His new fame as a sailing man came like that, almost by accident.

He had one short voyage in which he acted as the crew for a friend who owned a boat. He soon realised that if he was to have a boat of his own he would have to learn how to handle it. Yet he could not do this, unless he possessed a boat to handle. So he bought a small yacht called the *Florence Edith*. He hated the name, and, thinking of his experiences in the air, changed her name to *Gipsy Moth II*. She was really meant for day sailing, and was in many ways a pleasant boat to sail. He entered her for a race across the North Sea, from Harwich to Rotterdam. Mrs. Chichester thought he was sure to win, but he came in nearly last. This was in 1953. He still had a lot to learn about navigation.

He tried a race from Cowes in the Isle of Wight to Corunna. But this time he had a stroke of the bad luck which he had encountered when flying. The mast of the *Gipsy Moth II* snapped when they were close to the Channel Islands, and they limped somehow to Guernsey, under an emergency sail which they had fitted after clearing up the tangle caused by the broken mast.

He had joined a yacht club, and took part in a number of these races. At the end of the year he had sailed over two thousand miles, but thought that his racing record was the worst of any member of the club. At the end of the season, too, he went down with arthritis, and could hardly move. Chichester had become a vegetarian some time before, being advised to do this by a medical man, and now he went back to this man, had some treatment, and by the beginning of the next yacht-racing season he was fit again.

Now he had the great thrill of winning his first ocean race. This was from Southsea to Harwich, including a large arc across part of the North Sea. He had some highly skilled friends to help him in this race. But all the time Chichester was learning more about handling small boats, and he knew that, sooner or later, he would want to sail solo, his own master and his own crew.

A race from Cowes to Dinard was also a success. Mrs. Chichester had been with him on this race, and she was delighted to go up and receive the cup at the end of the journey.

The London business went on. But Chichester was now giving more and more of his time and attention to sailing. He had previously thought that there was no thrill as great as flying an aeroplane. He now came to see that a boat, though a far slower thing, could be just as exciting. The sea could be just as fascinating as the sky. It was no coincidence that when, in 1964, he came to write his life story, he called it *The Lonely Sea and the Sky*, for those two things had been the ruling passions of his life.

In 1955 he was beginning to become the master of the *Gipsy Moth II*, being able to control her in all winds and weather. Mrs. Chichester now went with him on almost all his trips, whether races or not, and was fast becoming as keen on this seafaring life as her husband.

There was, however, one terribly disturbing episode. In 1957 *Gipsy Moth II* and her owner were getting a reputation. She was entered for a number of races, and while she did not win by any means all of them, Chichester was getting a reputation as a bold and resolute sailor. But he had a number of illnesses, which he thought were caused by his being silly enough to go out in cold winds without enough clothes on. He had pleurisy, which sent him to bed. Then an abscess on his lung was found.

When he felt a little better, he went to Brighton for a short spell, hoping that the bracing air there would complete the cure. But he was still coughing, and a doctor friend whom he met at the seaside resort advised him to have his lungs X-rayed, just to make sure that there was nothing seriously the matter. He tried to laugh it off, but his doctor friend argued strongly in favour of the X-ray. In the end Chichester gave in.

The result was that it was decided that he had a cancer on his lung, and that it was in an advanced stage. More medical examinations confirmed this. He was told that the only hope was to have an operation for one lung to be removed.

This was a staggering blow. With minor exceptions, he had been healthy, and he found it difficult to think that he had one of the worst diseases known, and that he would soon have to face such a big operation as that which would cut out one of his lungs.

He told his wife. He told her, too, that he had arranged for the operation to take place on the following week. She thought that this was a mistake. She thought that if the lung were removed, it would kill her husband. She thought, too, that another doctor should examine him. This was done, and he confirmed the first men's findings.

Yet when he went into hospital and a detailed examination was carried out, the decision was not to operate, as the cancer did not seem to be getting bigger. A cancer grows in a human body and eventually kills the human being in whose body it is growing. But Mrs. Chichester did not believe that this was happening to her husband. She said that after the abscess his lungs were in such a state than an operation would set free poisons which would kill him. She would not allow the operation to take place.

There was one night when he was so ill that the doctors did not think he would survive. But survive he did. Then he went home, still feeling feeble and weak, but still alive, when most of the doctors thought he would be dead.

He had lost nearly three stones in weight. And when he summoned up the energy to go down to Devonshire to see his mother and other relatives they were shocked at his appearance.

On his return to London he was X-rayed again. The cancer had not grown. In fact, he was in better health than he had been months before. The doctors were mystified, but it began to seem as if he was recovering. And recoveries from cancer as advanced as his had been and are very few and far between.

They went to the South of France, hoping that this change would do Chichester good. In Vence, a very healthy town, they stayed. Here Chichester felt very ill again. But in the town was a very famous French lung specialist. He told Chichester that if he took the treatment he would prescribe he would be climbing the mountains again in a few days.

So it turned out to be. Mrs. Chichester thought that the disease was fading out before Chichester took the treatment of the French specialist, but that the doctor had given her husband confidence. Chichester himself thought that there was something which his body had needed, to stimulate the recovery, and that the French doctor had supplied whatever it was that was missing. Whichever of them was right, there was no doubt that he was cured. He had left England to all appearances a very sick man; he came back fit and well.

He had almost forgotten what he had learned about yacht navigation. But he soon picked this up again, and he was now often asked to take charge of other people's boats.

Then one day, in the yacht club, he saw a notice which announced a proposed race, solo, across the Atlantic. Ever since he had started sailing he had wanted to do with a boat the sort of thing he had previously done with an aeroplane. Would it be possible, he wondered, to take part in this? Was he now fit enough to face it? Certainly, he had never felt more fit in his life. His wife agreed that it would be good for him to try.

Three thousand miles solo! Would it be possible? Why not? Chichester grew more and more keen on the idea the more he thought about it. Those who wished to enter had to prove themselves good navigators by a preliminary test. They had to sail out to the Fastnet Rock and back. They had to do it solo, and only those who carried out this trip to the satisfaction of the judges would be allowed to take part in the race across the Atlantic.

The trip to Fastnet was not an easy one, and Chichester wondered if he would make it satisfactorily. He was now full of the idea of sailing across the Atlantic, which seemed likely to be the sort of exciting adventure which most appealed to him.

Many people were scared at this idea of a transatlantic race. It was thought that it might be very dangerous. A newspaper offered £1,000 first prize, and lesser prizes for everyone who completed the trip. This was an attraction, too.

Chichester by this time had a new boat, the *Gipsy Moth III*. She was designed for long journeys, with good cabins and with water-tanks to ensure the carrying of the large quantity of fresh water which would be needed on a lengthy voyage.

He decided that *Gipsy Moth III* should have her first real test on this voyage across the Atlantic. He had, of course, sailed a number of times on short trips, and proved a very satisfactory boat. She responded quickly to whatever her owner desired. He was very pleased with her, and he was sure that she would give a good account of herself when crossing the sea between Plymouth and New York.

In his early trials with her he found only one real difficulty. She was a good deal bigger than *Gipsy Moth II*, and this took a good deal of getting used to. She needed deeper water than the older boat, and this meant that on quite a number of occasions she went aground. She carried a dinghy, but she had high freeboards on her side. This made it very difficult to haul the dinghy on board.

Once, when sailing around the Isle of Wight, Chichester lost a dinghy owing to the yacht's high boards. He was towing the dinghy on a rope, and the rope snapped. He could see where the dinghy was, and he sailed close to her, thinking that he could pull the little boat aboard with a boathook. This took a lot of effort, and he soon found that he could not do this without losing control of *Gipsy Moth III*. He found, too, that if he was on a longish trip, where the need for sleep showed itself, he could not trust the boat to sail herself without his supervision. Before he could undertake any lengthy voyage, such as that over the Atlantic, he knew that he would have to fit some self-sailing gear.

He worked out this gear by watching model yachts on the Round Pond at Kensington Gardens in London. Model yachts, naturally, did not have anyone at the helm, and yet they could be so set by their owners that they would sail in some desired way. How was this worked? Would it be possible to fit a similar device to a full-scale big vessel? Chichester thought about this for a good while. Then he hit on a fairly simple solution. It was a sort of wind vane, which would control the way the yacht set herself to the prevailing wind.

When the vane was fitted, Chichester took the yacht

out into the Solent, off Southampton, selected an area where there were no ships near enough to be likely to cause danger, and set his vane for a course which he wanted the *Gipsy Moth III* to follow. To his delight the yacht sailed herself perfectly. If she veered the slightest bit off course, the self-steering device at once came into action, and she was at once brought back on to the course that he had intended. This, he said, was one of the most thrilling moments of his life.

He was ready to face the hazards of the transatlantic crossing. The main matter was to settle what he would have to take in the way of food and other stores. No one could be sure of just how long the voyage was likely to take, and it was no use getting the yacht into perfect racing trim, and then to run short of food before the journey was over. Chichester took potatoes and other vegetables, a hundred fresh eggs, and tins of stout and other drinks. He thought that this should be enough to keep his appetite satisfied for the long journey to New York.

Four men had entered for the race. When Chichester and his wife went down to Plymouth, where the race was due to start, he did not know an awful lot about the boats which were to be sailed by his rivals. One thing which he had kept quite secret was the route which he intended to take. A rule of the race was that the competitors could go by any route that they chose, as long as they started from Plymouth and finished in New York. Would it be advisable to try to go more or less straight across the Atlantic Ocean, or would they be more sensible if they made their way north for part of the way, and then turned southward somewhere in mid-Atlantic? These were the sorts of question which no doubt all the rivals asked themselves. But the answers they did not discuss.

The morning in June when they set out was cold and wet. There was a good deal of jockeying for position outside Plymouth, and at the start Chichester found that some of the others seemed to get away much faster than he did. This did not worry him. A few minutes gained or lost at the moment were of little importance. It was hours and days on the long haul that lay ahead that really mattered.

As he left the shelter of the breakwater in Plymouth Sound and made his way into the open sea, the weather grew rough, and heavy seas swept over the deck. In a very short time Chichester was soaking wet with sea water. One of the other competitors, David Lewis, broke a mast almost at the start. He put up an emergency sail and went back to Plymouth. Chichester afterwards commented that Lewis was the only man he had ever heard who broke a mast at the beginning of a race, and yet managed to finish third!

Chichester himself made steady progress. He got some sleep, thanks to his self-sailing device. But the first three days were very rough. There was a gale-force wind most of the time, and the waves were high and frightening. But he remained quite confident. *Gipsy Moth III* proved as reliable as he had expected her to be. She did all that could be expected of her, and her master was very happy at her performance.

His sailing device gave trouble now and then. More than once in the night, he would find that the lever which linked the tiller to the wind-vane had been knocked out, and as he scrambled on deck and looked at the compass he would find that she was sailing in the wrong direction.

Somehow he reached a stage at which he would wake up if there was any sudden direction change. Then he would dash up on deck and do the necessary corrections. But all this meant a certain waste of time.

For the first five days he found that he had averaged over 130 miles a day, which was good. But he had to tack a good deal, which meant that he was not doing anything like this distance in a straight line. The excitement declined as he got out of the rough area, and for some days all went smoothly. On June 25, when he had been at sea for a fortnight, he had gone over 1,200 miles— this time, calculated in a straight line from Plymouth. He had decided to keep as close to a straight line as he could, and not to veer too far either to north or south from this.

He had, naturally, no idea of how his rivals were faring. On that June day, though he did not know it, he had something like a two-hundred-mile lead over his nearest competitor, and the other two were even farther behind. David Lewis had lost nearly three days while the broken mast was being replaced, and was well behind the others, though he was now making good speed after that first mishap.

Chichester was making good speed too. He did not know what serious trouble lay ahead of him, though he thought that he could hear rumbles of thunder in the distance. There was a high wind, but it was in the right direction, and he thought that in a few hours, if he steered himself and did not rely on his self-steering device, he would be able fairly to scurry along, with a strong wind behind him.

He was getting sleepy. With this hint of storm in the air, he realised that it would be dangerous to take a nap, rely on his self-steering device, with all sails set. So he proceeded to haul down the sails. It was very fortunate that he did so. This was, however, easier said than done. The wind was now blowing at gale force, and the sails flapped madly as he struggled with them.

But by now Chichester realised that the wind was getting stronger. There was a really heavy storm building up. With much effort he had managed to get the bigger sails down, and he hoped that this would be enough to ensure safety in the difficult times that he was now certain lay not far ahead of him. The wind was blowing at sixty miles an hour, and, even with most sails down, *Gipsy Moth III* was fairly hurtling along.

He spent over five hours on deck, without a moment's respite. His automatic sailing device looked like breaking up, and he could not let go of the tiller for a moment. He grew afraid that one of the poles from the sails would break loose, swing overboard and make a hole in the boat's side.

Still the wind blew great guns. He had an instrument to measure wind speed, and it now registered 100 miles an hour. It must have been one of the worst Atlantic storms for years, and he was all alone in that little boat to fight it! The poles from the sails were lying about the deck almost in confusion, but he managed to tie the tiller long enough for him to get away and lash the poles down to the deck. It was the worst nightmare of a journey he had ever had.

Somehow, though, he survived and saw the *Gipsy Moth III* ride out the storm. In the cabin everything was flung about, and books and clothes were slung about in untidy heaps. Somehow he managed to snatch some sleep, though wondering all the while if the boat would keep on an even keel and maintain more or less the course which he wanted.

The next morning the wind had dropped somewhat. It was still strong, but not of the absolute nightmare strength that it had been. Within a few hours it had got better, and he was able to get some of the sails set again. He hoped that this would mean that the worst of the voyage was over. He was sure that if he struck anything worse he would not survive.

The work necessary to clear up the mess left behind by the storm was frightening. He worked, hour after hour, tidying up and repairing the damage that had been done. He had to climb up and repair a damaged rope. He was there, several feet above the deck surface, and wondering if he would ever get down again safely. Somehow this, as well as all the other hazards, were overcome.

He saw the great ocean liner, the *Mauritania*, pass. She was about a mile away, and Chichester wondered if the passengers in her luxurious lounges knew anything about the hardship through which he had gone.

Then he ran into fog, and had yet another disturbing experience. He saw, looming ahead of him, what looked like the outline of a giant man. Then he realized that his own shadow had been alarming him. It had been cast against the fog by one of the lights on his boat.

Soon, however, he left the fog behind, and he found that he was now getting more calm in himself. He was coming to terms with the conditions in which he was sailing. Still, he knew nothing of what his rivals were doing. He had not caught a single glimpse of either of them from the time when they had parted, soon after leaving Plymouth Sound.

On another night, about a week later, he awoke

suddenly, conscious that the *Gipsy Moth III* had veered off course. But again he scrambled up on deck, got some of the sails down, and so avoided the worst that might have happened as they struck another gale. This one was not, however, as bad as the one that he had previously ridden out.

There were well known to be fog banks at some spots in the Atlantic. Chichester had known of this, and had expected some 300 miles of foggy navigation. In the event, though, it amounted to nearly a thousand miles of it, and he got very weary of peering ahead of him, in an area of bad visibility, hoping that he would not hit some other seafarer in the foggy atmosphere.

Another danger which he dreaded even more than fog was the danger of icebergs. He was not crossing far enough north to be in the path of the worst of these. Yet there was always the possibility that one or two had drifted farther south than usual. If she hit an iceberg, his yacht would be finished. He had a radio set, and he would tune in to weather forecasts. But there never seemed to be any kind of information about Atlantic ice.

One day, much to his excitement, he found himself near to some whales. At first he could see only three or four of these giant creatures. But after a time he thought as many as a hundred of them were in view. He got the feeling that they were watching him, but as the *Gipsy Moth III* sailed steadily away they took little notice.

At the end of the fourth week of the race, Chichester had less than a thousand miles to go. He was able to speak to Christopher Brasher, who was working for the British paper that had originally sponsored the race. It seemed by this time that Chichester was well in the lead, and that his idea of making a journey not too far off the straight Atlantic crossing was paying off. The others, who had not tried to go direct, were well behind him. He could see the £1,000 prize nearly within his grasp.

He was now within sight of Nova Scotia, which meant that he had managed the crossing of the Atlantic, even though he was still a good distance from New York. He had some dangerous bits of coast to sail past. He was sure that would be easy going, after the storms and fogs he had endured. By the end of the thirty-seventh day he felt happy. It was the first wholly fine day he had gone through since leaving Plymouth, and the coast of the North American continent seemed deceptively near. Plymouth was now over 3,000 miles behind. It seemed like another lifetime, as he looked back at all that had happened to him since he had left the shores of Devon.

Very soon he sighted his first real landmark, which indicated that he was almost at his journey's end. This was the Block Island, at the entrance to Long Island Sound. He had only twenty-five or thirty miles to go— a mere fleabite compared to the thousands of miles that he had travelled. He tried to call the coastguards, and was then astonished to hear, over his radio, the news that his wife was there and wanted to speak to him.

When he finally crossed the finishing line that had been set as the end of the voyage, he had actually been travelling for forty and a half days. He had travelled 3,000 miles or thereabout in a straight line. The actual distance that *Gipsy Moth III* had covered was just over 4,000 miles.

He found Mrs. Chichester awaiting him, as well as Christopher Brasher, who was representing the newspaper. A wonderful feast was put on to greet Chichester, but he was so weary after his travellings that he went to sleep before he could finish the meal. Chichester had beaten the next successful competitor by no less than eight days, which showed that he was supreme as a navigator. It also showed the wisdom of his choice of course.

The voyage had attracted a lot of attention from papers all over the world, and, as soon as he had enjoyed a good night's sleep, Chichester found himself almost swamped with letters, telegrams and cables. His flights had made him famous enough. But that was as nothing compared to what now went on.

The journey home was something not very exciting to Chichester. His wife came with him, and they planned to go via the Azores. This would be a longer voyage than the outward one had been, but would be more pleasant. There would be less risk of storms, and it would be much warmer.

It was, in fact, too warm. As they approached the English coast Chichester was seasick—something that very rarely afflicted him. Eventually they landed at Plymouth. *Gipsy Moth III* had been nearly 8,000 miles since last leaving that harbour.

Again there came to Chichester the sense of having done something exciting and something worth while. But again—as with his flights—there was the feeling that now that the great journey was over everything was flat and dull. What should he do next? This was the question he asked himself at the end of 1960.

CHAPTER NINE

ON . . . AND ON

CHICHESTER had no real complaints about *Gipsy Moth III*. She had acquitted herself well. She had won her owner a prize of £1,000. So why should he grumble? He thought, however, of one or two possible improvements, and these he had put in hand during the winter of 1961-2. For one thing, he had often wondered if her mast would stand the strain of the transatlantic storms, so he now had a metal mast fitted, in place of the wooden one. This would give added strength. He also reduced the size of the mainsail, and had the smaller handsails made a little bigger. This should, he told himself, make her easier to handle.

Just what he was preparing the yacht for, he was not quite sure. He had ideas of entering for various races of one sort and another. His triumph in the race across the Atlantic had made Chichester famous, and he felt that it would be something of a comedown to enter for some quite ordinary race. His great aim in all such events was to get a sense of adventure, and there would not be much adventure in just sailing calmly around the coasts of Britain when he had done such longer voyages in the last few months.

By now Chichester was making a name, not merely as an airman and a yacht navigator, but as a writer. He had written several books. He wondered whether he could not undertake some new voyage, not merely for its own sake, but in order to write the story as he went along. In the end he found a paper that would pay him for a daily story via radio, if he tried the double Atlantic crossing—England to America and back again.

Boldly, he announced that he would set sail on June 1, 1962. It was a bold decision, because he still had a number of things that needed doing to the yacht. His automatic navigating device, while it had on the whole worked, was not as good as it might have been. He knew that he would have to improve its design. One of the oil companies designed special cans in which petrol could be carried on future voyages. He also arranged for crates of a brew of beer which he especially liked to be laid on. Mrs. Chichester now took charge of all the arrangements for food, drink, and stores for the two-way Atlantic crossing. This relieved her husband of a lot of the organising work, which he was only too pleased to leave to her.

Towards the end of May he took the yacht to Plymouth. This time he was not racing against rival competitors, but he was in a sense racing against time, as he planned to reach the American continent in thirty days, as opposed to the forty days which he had taken the previous year.

June 1 was fine and clear, very unlike the weather on which he had started in the race. The first day after leaving Plymouth was so good from the weather point of view that Chichester thought his luck was almost too good to hold.

This time he had planned to go a little further north. He knew that weather conditions varied a good deal from one part of the Atlantic to the other, and he hoped, by setting his course a little northward, to avoid the fog banks which had given him so much trouble.

He set the self-sailing device, laid down a sail on the deck, and then stretched himself out on it luxuriously, sun-bathing in the warmth. He had certainly not been able to do this last time!

He was amused when one day a homing pigeon landed on the deck. It was quite tame, though it would not allow Chichester to touch it. He fed it regularly and for a time it became quite a pet with him.

Two days out of Plymouth he saw the Fastnet light, at the south-west tip of Ireland, and recalled that a journey to that point had been the test before he had been allowed to take part in the race the year before.

This time he just gazed at it and sailed on. He phoned his story back to his paper each evening. His radio was working well. He listened to the weather forecast, wondering how long his luck would hold out and the weather continue to prove kind. On July 4 gales were forecast. He grinned to himself. The gales, surely, could not be as bad as those he had run into on his previous crossing this way.

The *Gipsy Moth III* rolled and pitched in the sea. Chichester was not seasick, but he did not feel quite well. The pigeon looked as if the motion of the yacht was giving him a lot of uneasiness. Chichester set the course and went to the cabin to prepare some food. While he was there he heard a loud bang from overhead. He dashed up on deck to find that a rope had snapped and one of the sail-poles was lying on deck. There was a horrible tangle of ropes on deck, which it took over an hour to tidy up.

By now he knew the dangers of these solo voyages,

and how badly the weather was liable to treat the lone traveller. On the next night the wind woke him. The sails were flapping and the wind roaring. The yacht was racing before an outlandish gale. The calm of his first two or three days had indeed proved deceptive. Now the Atlantic was getting its own back on him.

A day or two later, when he had thought that the gale had abated a bit, he found his automatic sailing device had temporarily failed, and the boat had completely turned around while he slept, moving swiftly back towards England, instead of onward towards America.

He had called up, on his radio-telephone, more or less at odd hours in the morning, as long as he got a story through to the newspaper in time for them to go to Press. But now he agreed that he would ring at a specified time each evening. Then they would know that he was all right, and also he would be able to see that his duty had been done, and would settle down to sleep, weather permitting.

An R.A.F. plane buzzed by, very close. Chichester thought that the pilot had done well to spot him, for the seas were now mountainous. The *Gipsy Moth III* was riding the heavy seas quite well, but Chichester had more or less shut himself in the cabin to keep dry and warm.

However, it occurred to him that the pilot might think that he was ill. When the aeroplane flew over at a very close angle for the third time, Chichester put his head out, only to get cold sea-water all over him. He knew, however, he would have to show himself, so he put on waterproof clothes, stepped up on deck, and waved a lighted lantern in signal.

Not long afterwards, the compass, which he kept on

the table of the cabin, began to behave oddly. He wondered what was happening. He appeared to be going
quite the wrong way. He was sure that he would have felt
this change in direction. But what was wrong? He had
been eating some shortbreads out of a tin, and he suddenly
had an idea. He pushed the tin along the table, and the
compass needle followed its direction. One would not
have expected that a biscuit-tin had been magnetic
enough to have an effect on a compass.

Since he was heading farther north than on his previous
voyage across the Atlantic, there was a greater danger of
icebergs, so he had asked his friend in the newspaper
office to get information about any known icebergs that
might lie anywhere ahead. This information was passed
on to him each evening when he had his talk with the
newspaper.

All sorts of minor mishaps caused trouble. He had
electric batteries on board. These were charged by a
motor which ran off an engine. Now one of the connector
belts broke. He could not go on using electricity for
light. He had to keep it for his precious radio set. So he
fell back on the paraffin lamps which he was carrying
as a kind of insurance against electricity failure.

Setting oil lamps as navigating lights was an awful
problem. Jerks would sometimes put the light out. But
he had to get one mounted in the rigging. He did not
think that he was very close to any main shipping lane,
but he did not want to sail without lights, and then
suddenly find some huge liner bearing down upon him.
He had thus to keep the paraffin lamp going somehow,
no matter how unpleasant the task might be.

It was all very difficult. He had, as yet, struck nothing
as bad as on his voyage the year before, but he had, after

all, no guarantee that he might not find something equally bad awaiting him.

Only a few hours after the heavy storm he ran into a period of almost complete calm, and *Gipsy Moth III* scarcely moved at all for quite a long time. By now Chichester was watching not merely the time, but the date as well. Would he achieve his aim of an Atlantic crossing in thirty days? It began to look as if he would not pull it off. He felt both worried and annoyed at the same time.

The pigeon had been company throughout the voyage. Chichester fed him on scraps of one sort and another, and found that he especially liked grated cheese. As cheese was an item of his own diet, there was usually a little to spare for the bird.

Chichester became afraid, as he drew nearer to the North American continent, that he was getting too far north, with the increasing danger of icebergs. He had heard the most terrifying tales of these huge lumps of ice, moving steadily through the water, and with far more beneath the surface that could be seen above it.

He tacked to the south, but found it difficult in the wind. When his actual sailing distance was seventy miles, he had moved only nine miles nearer to New York. This, he told himself, was no way to complete the voyage in thirty days.

Now another gale sprang up. It seemed, in whatever part of the Atlantic he might be, the danger of gales still existed. The yacht ran before the gale. He thought she was now going too fast, but did not know just how he could manage to slow her down a bit. The gale was so fierce that he grew afraid that she might be seriously damaged.

He had now got from London warnings of icebergs, though it appeared that the nearest was about ninety miles west. He decided that whatever happened he must not sail due west, or there would be real danger of hitting the iceberg. This again meant that he had to go a good way round. Once more he was losing valuable time.

He checked on the charts, and looked at the calendar. He had 1,400 miles still to go, and if he were to get to New York in thirty days from Plymouth, he had only ten days left to cover the 1,400 miles. He had to admit that it was very unlikely that he would succeed in doing this. The speed just was not possible, unless he could run before a gale blowing in precisely the right direction. And the likelihood of having that weather was not very great.

He was doing something between 130 and 140 miles a day. That made the thirty-day target just possible. But he did not think that he could keep up this speed for ten days or more on end.

When his thirty days were up, he was still over 500 miles from New York. He felt desperate, and yet he knew that there was nothing that he could do. Every day, now, he seemed to run into periods of calm. And when there was a wind, it was such a light one that he could not make much speed. He did not know if it was worse to have a gale or a calm. In a gale at least he was not losing a lot of time.

On July 2 he saw a buoy. He was now within striking distance of land. His wife, oddly enough, was almost above him. She had read all his despatches to the paper, of course, and flew over to New York, so as to be there to greet him. The aeroplane in which she was travelling passed more or less overhead, as he was preparing to get close to land. She recognized the boat, some five miles underneath her aeroplane. He had no idea that the speck in the sky was a machine in which his wife was travelling.

Soon now he could see Long Island. New York was not far away. He had failed in his thirty-day objective, but he had not failed badly. He rang up London and told the newspaper that he could now see a lighthouse ahead. This was what he thought of as his finishing mark.

In the middle of the night he reached New York. The journey had taken him a little under thirty-four days. It might be a failure in Chichester's eyes, but it was a glorious failure for all that. He had made the fastest crossing ever made of the Atlantic by a solo sailor. He had arrived on July 4, American Independence Day, and he was greeted by a telegram from President Kennedy congratulating him on a wonderful feat of seamanship. The next morning there arrived a cable from the best-known yachtsman in the world—Prince Philip, Duke of Edinburgh. If Chichester had been famous before, his fame had surely doubled as a result of this record crossing.

He spent some time with American friends, and then thought about the return journey. Mrs. Chichester was to come back with him. It was pleasant to have his wife with him, but he was never very happy at having her there, without someone to keep a watch. The automatic sailing device was something on which he did not mind depending for his own life; but he did not wish to risk his wife's life as well. His son Giles, sixteen years old, was with them too. But he felt that he could not ask either his wife, who was not well, nor a young boy, to take regular turns at the tiller. Most of the work, as before, fell on Chichester himself.

The journey was pleasant and less eventful than the outward journey had been. There were still gales to be faced, and Chichester grew more and more worried about his wife. Giles had bad spells too. Chichester thought that the boy was not cut out to be a long-distance yachtsman.

Yet before they did eventually reach England, Giles had become good at most of the routine tasks of the boat. Chichester did not know whether it was best to push on as quickly as possible, in order to get his wife ashore, or to go very slowly in the hope that the going would be less rough. He decided that he should compromise between the two extremes, going as fast as he could without risking really rough going, as he would have encountered if he had been racing, either against opponents or against time.

As soon as they left the shallow water off the American coast, and got over the Atlantic deep, however, she got better. Chichester felt much happier about her now. The later part of the journey was almost uneventful. They cruised along pleasantly, and when they eventually cast anchor in Plymouth Sound the journey (always faster in that direction) had taken just under twenty-seven days.

It was October. Winter would soon arrive. This was the time to lay up the boat, and settle down to building up his map-publishing business. He had done quite well with his newspaper contract, and now the articles which had been based on his radio-telephone conversations were made into a book, published under the title *Atlantic Adventure*. This, of course, covered only the journey from Plymouth to New York. But it gave a wonderfully fresh and lively picture of the journey which has been described in this chapter.

Writing, running a business—was it enough? For a year or two it was, though Chichester still entered for some races. He also toyed for a good while at getting another boat, which he knew would have to be called *Gipsy Moth IV*. *Gipsy Moth I* had been an aeroplane in which he had flown many thousands of miles, including that perilous trip across the Tasman Sea. *Gipsy Moth II* and *Gipsy Moth III* had been boats in which he had braved equally dangerous and difficult journeys. If he had a *Gipsy Moth IV* what would she do? It might be thought that now Francis Chichester had no more worlds to conquer. Flying record flights solo. Taking a small boat across the Atlantic. What remained to be done? As he sat in his office, taking down orders for maps, or as he wrote of his adventures, Francis Chichester wondered. He now had in his heart that great urge to travel, and to travel alone, his own master, his own pilot, his own navigator. He knew that there was something still awaiting him, though he was now of an age that most men are content to regard as the time for sitting back and taking things easily.

Chichester was never one to take things easily. The boy who had gone out to New Zealand, all those years before, had been a boy who wished to fight against the elements, who was never to be content to sit back and let life push him about. He would never be content to do that, at any age.

But what could he do now? What could he do that no man had ever done before, and that, maybe, no man would ever do again? Then, one day, an idea came to him. Why not a voyage around the world? A voyage, *solo*, around the world.

Long years ago Sir Francis Drake, setting out from

Plymouth Sound, had sailed around the world in the *Golden Hind*. Could another Devonian, setting out from Plymouth Sound, do the same thing, but this time do it alone, in a frail little craft, defying the winds and the waves?

No sooner had this idea come into Chichester's mind than he was starting to plan. It would have to be a bigger, sturdier boat than he had used up to now. The preparations would have to be very thorough, for he would no doubt be in remote spots, and would find that storms may be encountered in any part of the world. Preparations, thus, would have to be worked at for months—maybe for a year or two—before the voyage could even be planned. The boat had to be built, the stores had to be ordered. He would probably have to make some arrangements almost as complicated as those he had made for his long-distance flights years ago.

He would not, perhaps, have to land in savage places. He might be able to arrange at which ports he would call. But he would not be able to be quite as certain of dates as he had been when piloting an aircraft. A vessel which strikes storms and tempests, fogs and calms, cannot work to a timetable quite as an aeroplane does.

But soon he was getting down to the details of this epic voyage, which was to prove certainly the finest piece of seamanship for many generations. To go right around the world, solo, starting at Plymouth and ending at Plymouth—this was Francis Chichester's new objective. After that, it would seem that there could be little else on the surface of this globe which he could hope to attempt.

CHAPTER TEN

AROUND THE WORLD?

ON AUGUST 28, 1966, the *Gipsy Moth IV* left Plymouth. The objective was Sydney, a place which for Chichester had many memories. Over 13,000 miles he had to sail before he got there, and he was a little frightened, he confessed, at the prospect. He was also well over sixty years of age, which most people would have thought to be old to undertake a task of this magnitude.

Gipsy Moth IV was certainly the finest boat he had ever had. But she was small for work in the open seas. Only fifty-three feet long, she was built for lightness and speed. And speed she certainly achieved at the beginning. He was aiming at something over 130 miles a day. When he had been sailing for eight hours Chichester had done nearly sixty miles. That was good. But of course it had been on smooth water. From previous experience, he knew that he must expect to meet some choppy seas and probably some gales before he dropped anchor in Sydney Harbour.

The old sailing clippers which had done this trip in days gone by had taken, on an average, a hundred days sailing out, anything up to thirty days for refitting, and then another hundred days on the homeward voyage. Chichester hoped at least to equal these times. It was a bold ambition—perhaps the boldest of his life. But on all his voyages he would try to live one day at a time, only now and then giving a thought to the overall time-table.

His first great problem was to dodge, as far as he could, the Bay of Biscay. Everyone who has sailed around Europe knows the storms which are apt to take place there. A small boat would be tossed about wildly if she met the worst of these storms. *Gipsy Moth IV* was strongly built, but her size and her lightness would be such that too much rolling and pitching might cause serious trouble. Serious trouble so early in the voyage as that would be difficult to bear.

Rough water he found, as he had expected. As had happened so often before, Chichester had to tackle problems which needed quick solution. Almost at once some of the ropes which were used for an improved self-steering gear broke. Then Chichester's leg began to hurt. He wondered if he had badly pulled a muscle. It made it almost impossible for him to move about. Rapid movement was now necessary, in this early crisis, and he groaned as he found the boat pitching and tossing in the wild sea, which seemed to get rougher with every minute that passed. At the height of the storm there was a tremendous bang. He crawled below, to find that one of the bulkheads was cracked. Yet there was nothing that he could do about it.

Back on deck, he sat and waited. Soon the storm abated a little, and he could sense that the *Gipsy Moth IV* was still moving fairly smoothly. Soon all seemed to be well. He had escaped the storms of the Bay of Biscay without serious damage. The cracked bulkhead was sealed. He ate and drank comfortably now, having mended the lines of the self-steering gear. His one great trouble with his rations was that he had a barrel of beer which seemed to act in the craziest fashion. When he turned the tap there were occasions when no beer came out. At other times it would fizz and squirt all over the cabin floor. But as a rule he managed to get a drink of sorts.

For some days all went quite smoothly. After seven days Chichester found that he had done over a thousand miles, which was good going. When he had reached a little over two thousand miles, it was September 17—his sixty-fifth birthday. He smiled wryly when he remembered that this was the age at which many men retired and drew a pension. As he adjusted the 845 square feet of sail, he thought that he might be going into a Post Office to draw the first instalment of his retirement pension.

It was his birthday, after all, so he had to celebrate. It was the oddest birthday party he had ever had. Presents had been given him by family and friends before he had left Plymouth, and he now sat down, dressed in evening trousers and a velvet jacket, to open the parcels. He had a glass of champagne, and then went to bed, where he was soon sound asleep. He had been travelling in conditions of calm for several days now. But it was too good to last much longer.

The boat was hit by a sudden squall of wind. Chichester rushed up on deck, to find her almost out of control in the raging sea. He had to get the sails down somehow, or the wind might overturn the boat. It took two hours before he had managed to do this, and then he heaved a sigh of relief. It had been a curious end to his birthday celebrations.

Going around South Africa, he had decided to make a very broad sweep—getting nearer to the South American than the South African coast. This way, he thought, he would be likely to have better weather. But it meant that

radio messages were more difficult to send. He had
planned to keep in touch with London by wireless for as
long as possible, and then to switch over to the South
African stations, which would relay his messages to
London. He was writing, day by day, about his journey
to London papers, and so to keep in touch was important.
Likewise, he wanted to get weather information as
regularly as he could.

In seven weeks or thereabouts he turned eastward,
clearing the Cape of Good Hope and entering the area
sometimes known as the Roaring Forties. This part of the
sea is feared by all sailing men, and Chichester soon
knew why.

He struck the worst storm he had encountered on this
journey—a storm as fierce as some of the Atlantic storms
he had met previously, when racing to New York. The
wind howled, the sea roared. He had taken down all the
sails, and the *Gipsy Moth IV* was racing along under bare
masts. His self-steering gear was damaged again. He had a
sea-anchor, intended to keep the boat fairly steady when
far from land. He now threw this out, but the rope
snapped. He had lost the anchor and a goodly length of
rope with it.

He had a small sail, called a storm trysail, and in the
teeth of the gale he managed to set this. Now the ship
responded to the helm, and ran before the wind. Over
500 miles progress was made in three days, before the
storm died down a little, and Chichester managed to get
a little more canvas on the masts. He had snatched brief
periods of sleep during those three days, but had found it
in some respects the hardest three days in a life which
had known many difficulties and struggles.

He himself had fallen during this time, and had badly

bruised his ribs. His leg still gave trouble. With these mishaps he had to hobble around, cleaning up the mess which the storm had made, drying out the cabin, which was streaming with water.

The Roaring Forties had not finished with Chichester yet. He found himself being forced farther south than he had meant to go, and he knew that if he got down towards the Antarctic he might run into the danger of ice, which had caused him so much anxiety on his Atlantic crossing.

The worst accident yet took place on Monday, November 13, when he had been at sea for seventy-nine days. Another storm hit the *Gipsy Moth IV*. He struggled to the helm, and managed to hold the boat more or less on course. But when he examined the self-steering gear he found that it was so badly damaged that even he would not be able to repair it. He had nearly three thousand miles yet to go, and it began to look as if he would have to steer the boat by hand for the whole of the distance.

When he was almost in despair, he heard his wife's voice on the radio. She was coming out to Australia to meet him. He had thought of making for the nearest port for repairs, but now he decided to take a chance, and make for Sydney, in accordance with his original scheme.

It was a brave decision, especially in view of the fact that the self-steering gear was hopelessly out of action. Chichester, as always, was ingenious, and he managed to put together a temporary self-steering device with rope and a spare sail. It looked very much a haphazard and amateur piece of work, not neat like the original one. But when he let go of the helm and handed things over to his home-made steering device, he was glad to find that it worked reasonably well. So he would be able to sleep after all!

He was now drawing near to the west coast of Australia. To get to Sydney he had to go more or less around the Australian continent. He wanted to save time, if possible. So he decided to sail through the Bass Strait, which separates the island of Tasmania from the Australian mainland. This, too, was a brave decision. The Bass Strait is notoriously rough. Apart from the danger of rough seas, it is a very dangerous route, as there are a number of islands and jagged rocks, which make steering difficult. Chichester had maps and charts; but even so there was the constant danger of hitting a rock which might drive a hole through the frail side or bottom of *Gipsy Moth IV*.

Chichester had a speedometer on the boat, and he usually kept a fairly close watch on this. But when he was going through the Bass Strait, quite pleasantly sailing along, he suddenly had a shock. The speedometer dial went right off the end. In other words, the boat was moving at a speed greater than the speedometer would register! What on earth was happening, he asked himself?

Then he saw. A huge wave, driving towards the shore, had picked up the boat and was taking her shorewards, very fast. Is was like the surf-boards which skilful users are able to ride on, towards a sandy beach. The *Gipsy Moth IV* was being turned into a giant surf-board.

The boat swung round until lying broadside on the crest of the wave. She was tilted until the masts almost touched the water. Chichester knew that a matter of a few feet more of tilt, and the boat would capsize, hopelessly waterlogged. There was now nothing that he could do, except hang on and hope that she would soon right herself. This she did. He grabbed the tiller and got her back on to course. But it had been a near thing.

On his hundredth day he was in the Bass Strait. Then he headed for Sydney, with about 450 miles to go. Just outside Sydney he was becalmed, and he took the opportunity of tidying up the cabin and other parts of the boat.

He had known that his voyage had been watched with breathless interest all over the world. His articles had been printed in many papers. Pictures of his boat had been on television screens in many countries. But he now realized how many people had been following his progress.

He was within a few miles of Sydney, and countless vessels came out of harbour, their owners wanting to have a close-up view of *Gipsy Moth IV*. When he actually sailed into Sydney harbour, surrounded by Australian boats of every shape and size, he had actually taken 107 days from his departure from Plymouth. His wife was there to greet him, and he looked fairly fit and well (though thin). An Australian camerman took a picture of him, which was sent by radio to many countries. It was the first picture to be taken of him after his departure from Britain.

He was delighted to see his wife. His son Giles was there too. There seemed to be hundreds of journalists. Once inside the harbour, the Sydney Yacht squadron took him in tow, a policeman stood at the tiller, and Chichester and his wife toasted each other in a glass of champagne. When he came to step ashore he found himself very shaky on his legs. He had been so long on the moving surface of a boat's deck that the solid land seemed odd beneath his feet. People helped him. He looked, too, thin and haggard. He had lost a lot of weight during the perilous journey. He had to remember that he was really only half-way, and he emphasised this to the journalists and the men from radio and television programmes who crowded around him, anxious to hear in his own words how he felt after sailing alone for many thousands of miles.

He went to stay, with his wife and son, at a quiet little hotel in the suburbs of Sydney. He was not able altogether to dodge the newspaper men; but he knew that if he stayed in a big hotel in the centre of the city the limelight would play on him all the time, and he would not be able to relax and rest. And rest and relaxation were what he now needed more than anything else.

He wanted to consider the *Gipsy Moth IV*, and to decide if there was anything which needed altering before he set out on his homeward trip. The self-steering gear, it was sure, would have to be rebuilt. It was the serious damage to this which had caused him to lose time, and just to fail in his ambition to do the outward voyage in 100 days. He knew he would have to call in an expert to put this right.

This, and other repairs, were soon put in hand. It was not long before Francis Chichester was out in the boat again, sailing around Sydney harbour and trying out the *Gipsy Moth IV* after the work that had been done on her. He thought that, if anything, she sailed more effectively; but naturally there was a great difference in sailing around a fairly sheltered harbour and venturing out on the high seas. Moreover, he was planning to come back fairly close to South America, around Cape Horn. "Rounding the Horn" was always considered by the old sailing men as one of the most dangerous tasks in the world.

Then there was the job of loading with food and other

133

stores. These had lasted quite well on the outward journey, and he thought that something of the same amounts of food would be enough to see him safely back into Plymouth once again.

His wife and son helped with the checking of stores. He was given three bales of the finest Australian wool, which he was to hand over as a gift from Australia to the Prime Minister and the Lord Mayor of London. By this time no one thought for a moment that there was any possibility of his homeward journey failing.

He had landed in Sydney on December 12. On January 26 there came the most dramatic news that he had ever received. The Queen had decided to confer upon him the honour of knighthood, and sent him a cable of congratulation from Prince Philip and herself. Strictly speaking, he was not Sir Francis until the actually ceremony of knighthood, which could not take place until he arrived home, but everyone gave him the title in speaking and writing from that moment onwards. All seemed to realize that he had already earned it.

The day after receiving the news, Chichester went on board as usual, still working and still concentrating on getting every detail just right. He had planned to sail on January 28, and the fact of receiving such a signal honour from his sovereign was not enough to disturb the routine which he had worked out.

When the time came to sail, the harbour was full of craft of every kind, all intent on wishing him well. At seven o'clock he had breakfast with his wife—grape-fruit, scrambled eggs and coffee. He showed no signs of anxiety, no matter what he might have been feeling inwardly.

It was at eleven that he pulled away from the wharf of the Royal Sydney Yacht Squadron and made for the open sea—15,000 miles to go. There were hordes of photographers taking snaps of him, and he produced his own camera and took pictures of the photographers in return. Then he busied himself getting ready, setting the sails just how he wanted them. For the first hour or two his wife was with him. But she was taken off as he neared the open sea. She knew that she would not see him again for nearly three months, but she had every confidence that he would brave the dangers ahead, and so would complete what one journalist had called "the voyage of the century."

The first stage of the journey was to be across the South Pacific to Cape Horn. Sir Francis had worked out his voyage with the utmost care, and he knew that he had hazards to face. He had faced hazards before, and he was not scared. But he was not going to take any undue risks.

He planned to go south of New Zealand, before making for the tip of South America. He passed in this part of his journey very close to the edge of a cyclone. The Tasman Sea was almost familiar territory to him, and as he watched the progress of the yacht carefully, he thought of those days, now so far behind him, when he had flown the sky above. This was a very different sort of journey on which he was now engaged.

His first week at sea saw one storm after another. By now he was used to storms, and these for the most part, though nasty, were no worse than many that he had braved in the past. But then suddenly he was struck by the worst wind he could ever remember. The boat leaned over to one side, the masts touched the tip of a wave, and everything in the cabin was flung about wildly. Tins of fruit, potatoes and all the other stores fell out of their neat cupboards and rolled about. For a moment Sir Francis thought that the end had come. Then the boat slowly righted herself. He breathed again.

A hatch had burst open in the storm, and Sir Francis was swamped. The deck was awash and the neatly-stowed sails and ropes tangled badly.

He looked around him in alarm. He had a pumping system to get rid of any water. But he had not expected water in this quantity. It took several days to get it clear. And the mess in the cabin was indescribable. The stores were soaked and muddled. A cask of beer had been smashed, and he could smell beer in everything. The whole boat, which had seemed so neat only a few days before, was now in a state of complete chaos.

When the storm died down he started to tidy up. It was a heartbreaking task. Fortunately, he ran into smoother water, and he could set his course for Cape Horn, put the automatic steering gear working, and concentrate on the long and dirty job of putting all the stores back into their places. Some things, which were damaged hopelessly, he threw overboard. Luckily, the steering gear had escaped damage. If it had been smashed his position would have been very perilous indeed.

His course had to be worked out very carefully now. Rounding Cape Horn he had to keep at a fair distance from the shore, or he might be driven on to the jagged rocks which lurked close below the surface when any ship came in too close. Cape Horn, in spite of its name, is an island, and the currents which run around its complex series of channels have created dreadful hazards for the unskilled navigator who may come near to them.

Rounding Cape Horn was probably the most serious part of the whole voyage, and the newspaper readers of the world read eagerly the news, day by day, as Sir Francis approached it. Fogs, icebergs, submerged rocks— almost every hazard of the sea were there concentrated into one passage of a few miles.

This was, as Sir Francis afterwards admitted, the only part of the journey which really scared him, for he knew the dangers that were involved.

He snatched a few hours' rest before he drew near to the danger area. He was well aware that he could not trust the boat to his automatic steering device here. He would have to stay at the tiller himself the whole way round, no matter how long it might take him. As he awoke and made his way on deck he could see a swirling mist surrounding the boat. Conditions were as bad as they could be. He took a deep breath. This was it! If he could get through the next few hours all would be well.

As he sighted Cape Horn itself, he also saw a British ship, with the appropriate name of H.M.S. *Protector*, sailing close. He spoke to the captain on his radio, and was relieved to be told that there were no icebergs close ahead. That was one danger the less, at all events.

Then he spotted an aeroplane overhead. It flew low and he thought that pictures were being taken. Afterwards he learned that this was a machine containing both Australian journalists and men representing the B.B.C. The voyage had fired the imagination of the world. By this time everyone knew that the rounding of Cape Horn was the focus of danger which would take most overcoming.

The passage of the Horn was difficult. He had to hang on to the tiller like grim death. He had only a tiny wisp of sail, for he knew the danger of sudden gales which might capsize the boat if they struck her broadside on. He peered through the mist, hoping that no rocks lay ahead.

He had planned his route well. The *Gipsy Moth IV* sailed steadily onwards, passing through the danger zone almost without a shudder. Sir Francis wondered if he had been lucky or clever. Perhaps it was a bit of each. Before he knew it, he had rounded Cape Horn. It was time to make the long haul northwards, towards far-off Plymouth. He still had about 5,000 miles to go. But they should not be as difficult as the fifty miles he had now left behind him.

There was a yacht called the *Sea Huntress*. The B.B.C. and one of the English newspapers had chartered her, to go and meet Sir Francis, coming on the last part of the journey with him. They knew that he had hurt his elbow, and that it seemed that an abscess was developing. He took pain-killing pills for this, but could not take too many drugs, for fear that he might get very sleepy.

The journalists on the *Sea Huntress* sent a small boat across to the *Gipsy Moth IV*. With them they took a medical book which gave him advice on how to treat abscesses, as well as fresh bread and vegetables, but Sir Francis refused all supplies.

Coming past the Azores, he had fine sailing weather, with a strong breeze that was not strong enough to be dangerous. But three days out of Plymouth he ran into a period of calm. Now his messages to the Press did not mention his exact position. He was beginning to realize what a fuss would be made of him when he arrived, but he did not want the fuss to start while he was still at sea. He had no desire to sail in surrounded by other vessels.

Yet he could not refuse a naval escort.

Plymouth is, of course, one of the great naval centres of Britain. And Plymouth was to do him proud. On the Hoe —that great promenade high above the waters of the

Sound—thousands of people began to gather, as soon as it was known that he would soon be arriving. On the hilltops of Devon and Cornwall huge beacon fires were lit, as they had been years ago. The days of the Armada and the days when Napoleon threatened invasion were recalled, though this was a friend and not an enemy that they were celebrating.

By the time he approached the breakwater at the mouth of the harbour the thousands were cheering. By this time he was heading a regular flotilla of vessels of all kinds. They let him take the lead, and when he altered course slightly they all followed suit.

Nothing like this had been seen in Plymouth Sound before. Certainly not since the days of Sir Francis Drake had such excitement seized Plymouth. The original plan had been for Sir Francis to stop at the breakwater, but he would have none of this. He would sail right into Sutton Pool, the businesslike harbour of Plymouth.

A ceremonial barge took out Lady Chichester, her son Giles and Murray Sayle, an Australian journalist. Sir Francis greeted them warmly, and grinned when he saw that there were bottles of champagne with them.

The great voyage was over. After this everything was something of an anti-climax. Even the ceremony of knighthood, when the Queen, at Greenwich, dubbed him knight, paled into insignificance compared to the glory of that moment in Plymouth. The dinners in his honour, the presentation of congratulations by many bodies, meant little. He had set out to sail around the world, and he had done it! That was all that mattered. He had shown that, even in the twentieth century, when so many people seem to be turned out to a pattern, there is still room for the lone adventurer.

What will he do now? It would seem that he has no more worlds to conquer. But even as he approaches the age of seventy, it is difficult to imagine Sir Francis Chichester settling down to a dull old age. Even if he does nothing more, he will remain one of the greatest romantic heroes, not merely of the twentieth century, but of centuries still to come.

Author's Note

It is impossible in one short book to do justice to a man who has packed so much into one life as Sir Francis Chichester. The reader who wants to know more about him must be referred to his own books, of which the most notable is *The Lonely Sea and the Sky* (first published in 1964). *Atlantic Adventure* (1962) describes his crossing of the Atlantic, and *Gipsy Moth Circles the World* (1967) is his own story of his greatest feat of seamanship—his journey around the world.